MW01491385

Marco Island, Florida USA

Travel Guide and Tourism

Author
Bobby Chapman.

Publisher:
SONITTEC LTD
College House, 2nd
Floor
17 King Edwards
Road,
Ruislip
London
HA4 7AE

Table of Content

Summary

Travel around the world we live in?

1. (Traveling is easier than you think): We believe that traveling around the world shouldn't be hard: it's actually something everyone should be able to do at least once in their lives. Whether you choose to spend a few years or just a couple months traveling this beautiful planet, it's important to see what's out there. It's up to you to make the dream come true and take the first step. Launch Trip Planner to piece together and price your ideal route. Not sure where to start? You can always call one of our travel consultants and get some complimentary advice!

2.(Travel opens your eyes).: If you're open and willing, travel will make you an incredibly more well-rounded human being. And that's really the goal, isn't it? If you don't know where to start, check out our Around the World planning guide.

3. (Traveling helps you learn who you are).: All the challenges and opportunities travel lays at your feet help you discover who you are in a way that's only possible on the road.

4. (Travel creates meaningful relationships): People you meet while on the road become some of the most valued names on your contact list. They become places on the map to visit later on. These folks give you a glimpse outside your hometown circle of friends, and force you to take in new and refreshing perspectives, and ultimately realize that everyone is the same.

5. (Traveling develops skills you didn't know you had): Sometimes it's only far from home that you realize you you've got skills you've never used. It's travel that brings them to the surface and makes you smile, satisfied to have reached the mountain top, or crossed

a gorge or helped a villager clean up after a storm, or even to have successfully ordered a meal at a rural Chinese restaurant.

6. (Travel helps you learn new languages): There's something satisfying about being able to throw around a few words of Greek, knowing how to say thanks in Thai, pulling out that long dormant Spanish to book a room in Santiago, or simply hearing a language you didn't know existed just a few weeks before.

7. (Travel means adventure): Zip-lining over the jungle canopy in Peru, successfully navigating the maze-like streets of Venice, bartering for the best price in the traditional markets of Marrakech, taking a speedboat ride in New Zealand, or hopping in a Land Rover and heading out to watch animals grazing in Tanzania: these are adventures worth having. People are hardwired for the excitement of adventure and travel may just be the best way to tap into it.

8. (Traveling gives you perspective): Meeting people from other cultures will teach you that the way you've been looking at the world isn't the way everybody else does. In fact, your point-of-view might have some major blind spots. Seeing the world for yourself will improve your vision and your grip on reality.

9. (Travel helps you move forward): If you're between jobs, schools, kids, or relationships, around the world travel can be a perfect way to move from one of these life stages into your next great adventure. A big trip won't just ease your transition into the next stage of your life, it'll give you a chance to reflect on where you've been, where you're going, and where you want to end up.

10. (Travel is education): Seeing the world provides an education that's absolutely impossible get in school. Travel teaches you economy, politics, history, geography, and sociology in an intense, hands-on way no class will. Fortunately, the school of travel is always taking applications, no entrance exam required.

11. (Travel challenges you): Getting your daily latte at the same place and staring at your screen at your nine-to-five every day not nearly interesting enough? Even if you choose to work on the road (and keep staring at the screen), you'll have to find a new place to drink your latte, and depending on your destination, finding coffee, and foamy milk or a good place to sip them could prove to be a sizeable challenge. Travel is full of moments of joy and challenges. Overcoming the challenges gives you some of the greatest joys of all.

12. (Travel shakes things up): It sucks to be stuck in a rut. Everyone knows what that's like. A big trip can be your perfect solution. Fly around the world, stopping over in all of the places you've always wanted to visit. Go ahead and plan your ideal route around the world (it's easier than you think!)

13. (Traveling proves that dreams do come true): You imagined it, daydreamed about it, envisioned it. Guess what? It can be done. Around the world travel is possible, you just have to decide you're willing to take

the first step and start planning your itinerary. What are you waiting for? We've put together some specials to inspire you to live your dream.

14. (Travel gives you cool stories): Let's face it. Even for folks who can't tell a story, just the words "last year in Mongolia" get you instant party points. Even when events seem trivial, nostalgia and distance create an irresistible spin that makes mundane things like getting your laundry done in Zanzibar, entertaining. Just don't be that person and overdo it!

15. (Travel is literally food for thought).: You'll be constantly surprised at the flavors the world has to offer. The way people in other cultures and countries prepare food, and break bread together (not that all cultures even eat bread) will astound you.

16. (Travel gives you a sense of accomplishment): If you're the kind of person that dreams big, you're probably one to reach for new challenges. Finishing a trip gives you the satisfaction that you were able make

a goal to travel and accomplish what you set out to do see the world.

17. (Traveling for the hell of it): Why travel? Because you can. Because you want to. Because it beats the alternative (staying home). Why not pick up your tickets and get the ball rolling!

Introduction

Marco Island, the largest of Florida's Ten Thousand Islands, is tucked away in the Gulf of Mexico. It is a small, comfortable Island, 6 miles by 4 miles, linked to the mainland by two bridges. In 2014, Marco Island is voted the number one island in the U.S. and ranked it the fourth best island in the world. The largest on-line travel site went on to describe Marco Island as *"the perfect destination for those who crave a peaceful retreat."*

The Island has plenty to offer its visitors. There are many restaurants and outdoor actives for everyone: golfing, boating, fishing, world class shelling, water sports and much, much more. However, it's Marco Island's sub-tropical climate, pristine white beaches, and legendary sunsets that attract vacationers from all over the world. Watching a Marco Island sunset is a spiritual experience that touches one's soul for a lifetime!

Surrounded by preserves and uninhabited islands Marco Island is home to rare and endangered animals and bird species. Its many bays and undeveloped estuaries are fascinating to explore by kayak.

Fun fact: Where in the United States is the only place that alligators and crocodiles can cohabitate? It's the well-known Everglades National Park, a short drive from Marco Island. The Everglades' 1.5 million acres are swamped (no pun intended) with exotic birds, animals, plant life, and manatees that are all unique to the Everglades.

A Brief History of Marco

Crossing the Jolley Bridge and looking out over immaculately clean and incredibly manicured Marco Island dotted on the far end with high-rise condominiums glistening in the bright sun, it's difficult to imagine what the scene would have looked like in earlier times.

Before the times of bridges, condominiums, marinas and expensive cars, Marco Island was divided into two different land masses; an area that is now the southernmost third of Marco and an area of about 50 acres of shell that had been raised by hand by Calusa Indians, who came to the Island at an unknown time and disappeared around the time of the Spanish

Explorers. It was this northern tip that was named Key Marco and is now known as Olde Marco.

What is now the "center" of Marco Island was nonexistent. It was a water outlet into the Gulf of Mexico until it later became a mangrove swamp.

The Mysterious Calusa

What attracted a tribe of Paleo-Indians to Marco Island? That is a question that remains shrouded in mystery, as relatively little is known about this group of fishermen and skilled artisans who lived on Marco for perhaps more than a thousand years.

As tourists and residents of today, the Calusa were likely drawn to the island for its tropical, sheltered, almost mystical atmosphere. They were thought to have considered Marco a sacred place, as storm clouds rolling towards it often seemed to stop mysteriously and travel north or southward.

The Calusa were accomplished fishermen and artisans. They made brightly painted clay masks to resemble animals, they carefully wove fishing nets, they were known as fierce warriors and they wore jewelry and clothing - albeit very little in such a climate!

The Calusa also practiced an early form of recycling. They build giant mounds using clam shells, fish bones and other discarded items. The shell mounds located in what is today the Indian Hills area of the Estates are still today the highest area in Collier County. A new generation of twentieth century homes occupy the area.

It was believed that the plight of the Calusa was unfortunately similar to that of so many other Indian groups. European explorers such as Ponce de Leon, who may have died close to Marco after a battle with native people, brought disease and weapons with them. The result was decimation.

Captain Bill and The Cat

The arrival of homesteader Captain W.D. "Bill" Collier rang in the arrival of "civilized" life on Marco in 1870.

Collier's Marco Island centered around the fishing and clamming industry. Captain Bill's relatives still live on Marco Island today..Three of the original building of Collier's sleepy village still remain in the Olde Marco area today and receive more activity than they did in Collier's time. They now are all popular restaurants!

Captain Bill stumbled upon one of the richest archeological finds in Florida accidentally while he dug mucky soil as fertilizer for his garden. After word got around and the Smithsonian Institute archaeologist Frank Hamilton Cushing got involved in the excavation, which later became known as the widely celebrated "1896 Expedition",hundreds of artifacts were uncovered. Unfortunately, many of the items were lost days, sometimes hours, after being exposed to the air outside their mud burial site

One six-inch wooden brown-red cat statue did, however, survive. The Key Marco Cat, as it was later dubbed and is still called, became the very symbol of the lost Calusa and remains so today.

From November 1995 to May 1996, the feline made a special centenary appearance at the Collier County Museum. On loan from the Smithsonian reserves, it struck wonderment into the minds of thousands of visitors.

Barron Collier's Dashed Dream

Barron Collier, a wealthy Northerner, inventor and generally well-respected forefather of the county that today shares his name, had a grand vision for Marco Island. However, he never quite realized his wish to develop and "vacationize" Marco, as he was unable to buy out Captain Bill and have complete control of the island. The depression of the 1930's certainly didn't help matters either. The failure of Barron Collier's Marco vision set the fateful stage for other broken dreams and land squabbles.

Deltona Days

The isolated, mosquito-infested and largely undeveloped little island remained so up until the early 1960's when Barron collier's last holdings were sold to

Deltona Development Corporation with brothers Elliott, Robert and Frank Mackle at the helm.

The rich and famous as well as the blue collar were drawn to the "Hawaii of the East" by an incredibly successful marketing campaign. A beach-front hotel lured guests onto the sandy, clean and pristine beaches of Marco. Affordable subdivision-like housing was bought by those wishing to own a piece of paradise on the island's eastern shore, which was soon connected to land by a bridge. Many of these original homes are still occupied today by Islanders.

The Army Corps of Engineers, who had briefly held a post on the southern tip of the island during the 1950's at a missile tracking station, became embroiled in a lawsuit with the Mackle brothers when Deltona mapped out its development plans to include lands the government had deemed "environmentally sensitive."

After years of expensive court battles, the Mackles admitted defeat, but Marco Island would forever e indelibly etched in the minds of many as the ultimate vacation and living atmosphere.

Today and Tomorrow

Today it is a well established fact that Marco Island is a first-class resort island with a unique atmosphere that simply can't be found elsewhere. Where else would one find millionaires sitting among fishermen at chickee bars drinking and talking about the incredible fishing that can be had any time of the year?

Widespread development has brought multimillion dollar homes and condominiums, four-star resort hotel complexes, stores catering to all tastes and styles and a truly delightful assortment of restaurants. It has also brought a yearly influx of seasonal visitors who long to "run to the sun" when northern winters bring the chills.

Some would argue that development has brought congestion, noise and inevitable environmental destruction. But Marco Islanders, like the citizens of any precious community, take pride in their island. Various organizations have gotten involved in Marco's development - and it's only about 48 percent developed at present. Islanders are watchdogs, becoming politically active in an attempt to preserve the little Florida island history has shaped into a true paradise.

Travel and Tourism

At the northern tip of the Ten Thousand Islands and 18 miles south of Naples, Marco Island serves as a large playground for sun seekers and outdoor sports fans.

Although the island is lined with contemporary high-rise hotels and resorts, most of the attention is focused on its beautiful beaches and the Gulf of Mexico. Crescent Beach spans the entire 3.5-mile length of the island along its western coastline and is covered with velvety sand the color of alabaster. Hotel guests can rent jet skis, sailboats, kayaks and equipment for parasailing and windsurfing along most of Crescent Beach, which is fronted by hotels and condominiums.

Tigertail Beach, a 1-mile section of Crescent Beach at the island's northern tip, is accessible to all visitors. There's no danger of boredom here; you can rent all sorts of beach gear, including lounge chairs, umbrellas, kayaks and a 7-foot-long watercraft called a Sea Squirt, which shoots 20-foot-tall sprays of water. There also are showers, a playground and a beachside café in case you're hungry for a juicy burger or a veggie wrap. The beaches also are known as a shell-gatherer's paradise; scan the sands for such varieties as sand dollars, scallop shells and whelks.

Marco Island also is home to more than 100 miles of waterways, luring boaters and fishermen; the island has several marinas from which to launch your craft or a rental, including Rose Marina; phone (239) 394-2502. From late December to late April (also Tues.-Wed., early July to mid-Aug.), Key West Express, 951 Bald Eagle Dr., offers a ferry service to Key West for a fee (weather permitting); phone (888) 539-2628 to confirm schedule.

Long before Marco Island became a resort area, it was home for hundreds of years to the Calusa Indians, a fierce tribe whose main food source came from the surrounding waters. As a result, the Calusas left behind many shell mounds as well as other artifacts. The most well-known is the 6-inch-tall Key Marco Cat; carved from buttonwood, it has a mixture of human and panther features and may have been used for religious practices. The figure now is housed in the Smithsonian National Museum of Natural History in Washington, D.C. The Marco Island Historical Museum, displays a replica of the Marco Cat

Exploring Marco Island

Water Sports, and More
Marco Island restaurants, resorts, entertainment and shopping offer an unparalleled opportunity to have a luxurious yet affordable vacation experience. This vibrant waterside residential community, with all its amenities, is set against the backdrop of the unspoiled natural beauty of the Gulf of Mexico, the 10,000

Islands and the Florida Everglades, creating an island destination which is totally unique. That's why ew are ranked the NUMBER ONE Island in the USA, and NUMBER FOUR in the world in 2014!

Situated approximately 100 miles west of Miami and 180 miles south of Tampa, Marco is the largest and most northerly of the 10,000 islands. It is connected to the mainland by two road bridges: the Judge SS Jolley Bridge to the north and the Goodland Bridge, now know as the Stan Gober Bridge, to the south.

Just six miles long and four miles wide, Marco Island's climate is semi-tropical with an average year-round temperature of 74 degrees. (Even in high summer it never reaches more than an average of 91 degrees, although the high humidity does make it feel hotter than that.) We have an average annual rainfall of 49 inches, which occurs mainly in the summer and early fall. The average water temperature of the Gulf in January and February is in the low 60s; in April, May,

November and December it is in the 70s; and it reaches the low to mid 80s between June and November.

With the exception of a few small industries, such as pineapple growing and clam canning, Marco Island remained pretty much undeveloped until the early 1960s. In 1962 the Mackle brothers, of Deltona Corporation, developed a master plan which involved the construction of 91 miles of canals, complete with seawalls, to make Marco the beautiful waterside community it is today. The first Deltona sales office opened on Marco Island 51 years ago this January so Modern Marco is celebrating its 51st anniversary this year.

Marco Island was incorporated as a City in 1999. Our population fluctuates between approximately 17,000 in the summer and around 40,000 in the winter months.... our "season."

Attractions include around a hundred restaurants and several great shopping centers. But, as we are surrounded by the pristine waters of the Gulf of Mexico and the tranquil backwaters of the 10,000 islands, water sports and beaches are the main draw of a Marco Island vacation. Activities such as world class sport fishing and exceptional eco-tours head the list of things to do on Marco Island, closely followed, of course, by golf.

Let's not forget the incredible wildlife, which includes dolphins, osprey, herons and many endangered species like the bald eagle and the manatee. Then there's the beautiful five mile natural crescent beach, which is world famous for its wonderful shelling. While walking the beach in spring and summer you are likely to sea turtle nests and thousands of shore birds nesting on the spit of land that separates Tigertail Lagoon and the Gulf.

And last but not least, Marco Island is also known as the gateway to the Florida Everglades. Just a short drive away, the Everglades National Park, which lies between Marco Island and Miami, covers 1.5 million acres and is the second largest park in the lower 48 states

With all this and more to offer, why would you go anywhere else? Start planning your Marco Island vacation today!

Marco Attractions

The Beach

Marco Island's beautiful crescent shaped beach stretches the whole length of the west side of the island.

Of course the beach is public property and open to all and, unless you're staying in a beach front hotel or condo, there are three main access points to the beach... Tigertail Beach, South Beach and Residents' Beach (which is only accessible to residents who are members of Marco Island Residents' Beach).

We thought it might be helpful to talk a little about them....

Tigertail Beach

The most northerly beach access point, Tigertail Beach, can be reached by taking either Tigertail or Kendall

Dr from North Collier Blvd and then turning left onto Hernando. Parking is free for Collier County residents

who display a permit and for all other visitors it's $4 for 3 hours and $8 for all day. If you speak to the gate staff you may be able to get just a one hour rate.

It is best to consider Tigertail Beach as two quite distinct areas, the Lagoon and Sand Dollar spit.

The Lagoon Great Family Fun

You approach the lagoon from the parking lot via one of six walkways and there is a rest-room at the furthest

walkway. Once on the sand you will be looking west towards Sand Dollar Spit and beyond to the Gulf of Mexico, which is hidden from there by seaoats, shrubs and even some small trees. The lagoon is a great place for families with younger kids to spend the day since it is normally very calm and the concession rents cabanas - a must if you are going to spend much time out in the hot Florida sun. In addition, you can rent aqua-trikes, paddleboards and all kinds of kayaks, including fishing kayaks.

One really neat trip is to kayak or paddleboard along the lagoon and access many of the small mangrove inlets and then beach the kayak on Sand Dollar Spit for some wonderful shelling. It's best to go a couple of hours before high tide for maximum access. If you are an avid photographer, you can also sneak up really close to the herons and ibis, as they rest in the mangroves or feed in the shallows. All of the rentals are either pedal, paddle or electric and do not interfere with the peace and quiet.

Observation Tower and Fantastic Wildlife
The lagoon is also a great place to fish (either spinning or fly) with many secluded areas around mangroves or shallow water towards the Big Marco Pass. Over the years it has become an important rest area for

migrating birds and also a major nesting site in spring and summer for several endangered species, like the least tern and black skimmer, and is listed as Site # 73 on the Great Florida Birding Trail. You can expect to see many types of heron, ibis, egret, plovers, sandpipers, willets, pelican, osprey, roseate spoonbills, and even a bald eagle. There are always mullet jumping and you should also see fiddler, horseshoe and ghost crabs and maybe three kinds of sea stars depending on how far you walk! The Observation Tower, with two levels and permanently fixed telescopes, gives unobstructed views of the lagoon and out to Sand Dollar Spit as well as an eye level view of a nearby osprey nest. The tower is handicap accessible from the main walkway close to the snack bar, and is open from dawn til dusk.

Café and Playground

The great benefit to this part of Tigertail Beach is that you are also close to all of the facilities -   restrooms, showers, BBQs, a great kids' playground and the café that offers lunch and light snacks, beverages and ice cream. Kids' meals come with a beach frisbee, ready for fun in the sand.

Sand Dollar Spit a Magnificent Unspoiled Gulf Beach
To reach Sand Dollar Spit and the beautiful, pristine, soft sandy beach on the other side of the lagoon, you either have to wade through it, head south some distance to where the lagoon ends and make a turn to the north, or rent a kayak or paddleboard and make it part of a day trip. It's a bit of a trek to walk to the spit, but it's definitely worth it. The beach here (which abounds with wonderful seashells) is absolutely breathtaking and totally natural.

The walk to the end of Sand Dollar Spit has changed many times and no more so than in September 2017, due to the impact of Hurricane Irma. The spit is so narrow in a number of places that breaches can occur, especially after strong tides. If on your walk you reach an area where the gulf is flowing into the lagoon, do be aware that not only could it be fast flowing, but if it is an incoming tide it may be a lot deeper on your return.

Many of Florida's beach-nesting shorebirds that face conservation challenges can be regularly spotted on Sand Dollar Spit and Tigertail, including the snowy plover, least tern, black skimmer, American oyster catcher, and Wilson's plover. So please keep your distance and never intentionally force birds to fly or run.

Respect posted areas and don't feed wildlife.

No two visits are ever the same and you can walk for miles with just the lapping of the waves, the rustle of the seaoats and the cries of birds to keep you company. In our view it's the best part of the whole beach and is well worth the walk, but don't forget to take some water with you (it can get pretty warm out there!) and some shelling bags since there are over 200 different shell varieties that can wash up on these shores.

Residents' Beach

Reserved exclusively for island residents who are members of the Marco Island Residents' Beach, this beach park is nothing short of sensational. With a multimillion dollar beach pavilion, café and children's' play area, the facilities here are second to none. If you're considering buying a home on Marco Island ask your realtor to take you there because a visit to Residents' Beach should certainly help to make up your mind.

Everything is beautifully kept and absolutely pristine. The parking area (which is also for members only) is separated from the beach by wide sweeping lawns which are liberally scattered with Queen Palms and flowering shrubs. Many large chickee huts provide shade for family gatherings around the picnic tables and BBQs. It's an easy walk across the boardwalk to the soft white sand where more chickees offer shade for members. There's even a large raised viewing area for the disabled and a beach wheelchair is always available.

Residents' Beach is located in the center of the beach at the intersection of Collier Blvd and San Marco Road. Walking south from here will bring you to the more populated areas around the hotels, time shares and condos, while walking north will take you to the unspoiled area west of Tigertail Beach previously described.

Residents' Beach also has a members only parking lot close to the South Beach public access on Swallow Avenue, just off South Collier Blvd. There are bathroom facilities and a nice grassed area with Chickee huts, a children's slide and BBQs.

 If you own improved property on Marco, or rent for one month or longer you are eligible to join Residents' Beach.   Call 642-7778 for membership details.

South Beach

Located right at the southwest corner of the island, the South Beach parking lot on Swallow Avenue is a short stroll across Collier Blvd and through a recently updated tree lined walkway to the beach. Parking is free for Collier County residents who display a permit, and $8 for all other visitors. Parking is limited, and a strictly enforced fine of $95 will be issued for cars parked anywhere but designated parking spots, even surrounding streets and swale areas.

The public restrooms in the parking lot are the only facilities although beach chairs, umbrellas, kayaks, hobie cats and windsurfing rentals, are available for rent along the beach. Sunset Grille Beach Bar and Restaurant, which is located in the Apollo condominium (the yellow building just north of the beach access), is open to the public from 11am and is easily accessible from the beach for a casual lunch or dinner.

South Beach is a wonderful place for shelling, beach fishing and dolphin watching and is the most suitable beach for parents with young children or anyone with lots of beach things to carry. There is a drop off point at the access on S. Collier Blvd. If you are looking for a different way to experience the beach, check out Marco Island Yoga's schedule on the Marco Review App.

More Beach Info...

If you want to reach the central beach, Turtle Lot is a 90 space privately owned public parking area on S. Collier Blvd opposite Charter Club with access to the beach via the public walkway just north of Crystal Shores. The cost is $12 per day and there are signs directing visitors to the beach, by crossing S. Collier Blvd at Winterberry Drive and then walking south. There is an additional access walkway to the beach just north of the JW Marriott, but because there are no parking facilities (with the exception of two bike racks), it can really only be used by those staying within walking or cycling distance.

Please remember that pets and cycling are not allowed on any of Marco Island's beautiful beaches and that all public beach access points are only open between dawn and dusk so, unless you're staying in a hotel or condo on the beach, a moonlight stroll on the sand is unfortunately not an option.

Nearby Beaches

The many uninhabited islands south of Marco offer the opportunity to really get away from it all as they are only accessible by boat or personal watercraft. You can get to them either by renting a boat from a local marina or taking one of several local eco boat tours. Hemingway Water Shuttle, offer a regular service from Rose Marina to Keewaydin, a sparsely inhabited barrier island just north of Marco with a wonderful eight mile long sandy beach. You can rent beach chairs from them and there are food and ice cream boats which service this island too so it makes for a great family outing.

However you choose to get to the beach have fun in the sun and don't forget your sunscreen and to leave behind only your footprints!

Shells

With all the wonderful shells literally 'there for the taking' on our beautiful beaches you're bound to come up with a few you don't recognize, so use our Beachcombers' Guide to identify your treasures. You'll find great shells all along the beach but the area right at the southern-most tip is particularly good as is the area between the gulf and the south tip of the lagoon at Tigertail beach. The north part of the beach is the best place to look for sand dollars. We also have a great store on the island where you can buy all the supplies you'll need to preserve your finds and pick up ideas on how to incorporate them into wonderful hand crafted gifts and keepsakes.... You can buy local shells there if you don't want take the time to find them yourself, and they also have great selections of amazing shells from all around the world. Shore Goods, in Marco Walk Plaza (which used to be known as Marco Craft and Shell Company, and located in Marco Town Center Mall). 239-394-7020

Botanical Gardens

NAPLES BOTANICAL GARDEN - A unique 90 acre sanctuary with several different eco-systems. The Preserve's giant pines and ancient cypress, unspoiled marshes and twisted mangroves provide vital habitat for hundreds of species of animals from bald eagles to otters and tree frogs to gopher tortoises. 4820 Bayshore Drive, Naples. 20 minutes from Marco - US41 North towards Naples, turn left on Thomasson. 643-7275

Museums & Galleries

Marco Island Historical Museum - Providing a glimpse into the unique past of our area this beautiful new museum is now almost complete. It features the

Calusa Gallery which traces Marco's history from its geological formation, through the times of the Archaic Indians, the Muspa and Calusa Indians and the discovery of the world famous Key Marco Cat.. Another exhibit details the development of Modern Marco and a third exhibit, the recently opened Pioneer Room, is an interactive exhibit which chronicles the evolution of the pioneer villages at Marco and Caxambas and offers visitors an in-depth look at the poeple, industries and lifestyles on Marco Island during the late 1800s and early 1900s.

The Windows & Doors to History exhibition, which has also recently opened, is one of a kind, featuring 24 faux windows and doors depicting vivid scenes spanning 6,000 years of Marco Island history from the Pleistocene, Archaic, Glades and Calusa periods to the pioneer period and modern Marco. Original works of art were created by seven renowned artists for transfer to the faux windows and doors that encircle the outside walls of the Museum complex buildings.

Participating artists are John Agnew, Paul Arsenault, Merald Clark, Muffy Clark Gill, Tara O'Neill, Jarrett Stinchcomb and Malenda Trick.

The museum has recently been given approval to bring home on loan some of the Key Marco Calusa artifacts, including the Key Marco Cat, excavated during Frank Hamilton Cushing's world-famous 1896 archaeological expedition.   Hopefully these items will be on display from mid-November 2018.

There's also a great little gift shop and other traveling exhibitions so this museum is definitely worth a visit and a great rainy day activity. Open Tuesday-Saturday 9am-4pm. 180 Heathwood Drive.

Marco Island Center For The Arts - Art galleries, classes & workshops as well as a gift shop featuring local artists' work.. . 1010 Winterberry Dr. 239.394.4221

Parks & Preserves

Big Cypress National Preserve - Over 700,000 acres of cypress swamp and sawgrass prairie which is home to

many endangered bird species and the Florida panther
- 45 minutes from Marco.

(239) 695-4111

<u>Collier-Seminole State Park</u> - 7,200 acres wilderness preserve. Camping and RVs, canoe rentals, guided canoe tours Mondays, Wednesdays & Saturdays, boat ramp, guided night hikes, 6.5 mile hiking trail, self guided nature trail on boardwalk and interpretive Center. 20200 E. Tamiami Trail, Naples. Take San Marco Road to US41, take right towards Miami and its on your right - 15 minutes from Marco. 394-3397

<u>Corkscrew Swamp Sanctuary</u> - National Audubon Society owned 11, 000 acre nature preserve. 2¼ mile boardwalk through primeval swamp & virgin cypress stand. See wildlife - alligators, birds (nesting wood storks) etc at close quarters. Wheelchair accessible. Take SR951 to Immokalee Rd and head east - about 1 hour from Marco. 348-9151

Ding Darling Nature Reserve - See rare birds up close without even leaving your car! It's about 90 minutes from Marco on Captiva Island but it's worth the drive. Take exit 131 from I75 and follow signs for Sanibel and Captiva.

Everglades National Park - The third largest national park in the US. The closest visitor center to Marco is in Everglades City, where there are boat tours, orientation films and camping 45 minutes from Marco. (800) 445-7724

Fakahatchee Strand State Preserve - 32,000 foot long boardwalk and hiking trail through virgin cypress in the major drainage slough of southwestern Big Cypress Swamp. The original bald eagles' nest which was visible from boardwalk was destroyed by Hurricane Irma but they have built a new one nearby. This is a great place to see alligators up close and personal, including baby alligators and lots of other great wildlife. Nesting bald eagles are visible from boardwalk. US 41 just before turn off for Everglades City - 25 minutes from Marco. 695-4593

The Conservancy's Naples Nature Center-Wildlife Rehabilitation Center, The Conservancy Museum of Natural History, Nature Store, 45-minute guided boat tours, guided trail walks, canoe & kayak rentals. 14th Avenue North, off Goodlette-Frank Road, Naples - 35 minutes from Marco. 262-0304

Koreshan State Historic Site - Guided walks at site where Cyrus Reed started a religious community. Also boating, fishing, picnicking, and nature study. US41 at Corkscrew Rd - 50 minutes from Marco. (239) 992-0311

Frank Mackle Community Park - Walking, biking, playground, picnic area, soccer, bocce courts, shuffleboard, and indoor games room. Kids' spray park & two dog parks. Andalusia Terrace, (off S. Heathwood). 642-0575

<u>H P Williams Roadside Park</u> - Picnic tables, rest rooms, and a safe viewing platform to watch alligators, fish, turtles and birds. Carry on along Turner River Road, with the drainage canal running alongside, to see more alligators and abundant bird life just feet from your vehicle. On US 41, 6.6 miles after the turn to Everglades City.

<u>Janes Scenic Drive</u> - 11 mile drive on an old hard-packed Cypress logging trail through the Fakahatchee Strand State Preserve. See bromeliads, alligators, herons, deer, turtles, and butterflies. Park and venture on foot down one of the old logging trails. US41 to SR29, turn left, approximately 2 miles on left.

<u>Marco Eagle Sanctuary</u> - Site of nesting bald eagles since 2003, with adult eagles remaining on the sanctuary property year round. Regularly seen early morning and late evening before dark. The eagles were late nesting this year but now have 3 chicks in the nest. 665 Tigertail Ct.

Rookery Bay Environmental Learning Center - This facility offers hands-on exhibits and live specimens of the plants and animals that inhabit Rookery Bay, the 110,000 acres of pristine mangrove forest area just north of Marco. 300 Tower Road, off 951, just south of SR41. 20 minutes from Marco.   417-6310

10,000 Islands National Wildlife Refuge - This 35,000 acre refuge is largely wetlands but visit the one mile trail and observation tower to see wildlife and tranquil views across the prairie and swamp grass. Best at sunrise and sunset. Take SR92 to US41 and turn right towards Miami. Approximately 2 miles on right.

Zoos

Naples Zoo - 52-acre botanical garden founded in 1919 with animals from apes to zebras including the big cats. Presentations throughout the day and a boat cruise through islands of monkeys. Allow a half day to tour zoo. 1590 Goodlette-Frank Rd. Naples - 35 minutes from Marco.   262-5409

Shopping Centers

We're only a small island, but Marco offers great shopping with lots of great one-of-a-kind stores... we have everything covered right here so there's no need to go further afield. There are many small malls and stand alone shops dotted around the island but our main shopping centers are:

An up-market shopping and dining area on North Collier Blvd which backs onto Smokehouse bay and offers a marina, three restaurants with waterfront open air seating and an open air bar which often has live entertainment. It is also home to two great ladies' clothing and accessory stores, a ladies' shoe shop and it also has yacht sales, a yoga studio and ice cream parlor.

Island Plaza

Located on the north west corner of the intersection of N Collier Blvd and Bald Eagle Drive this plaza houses an outlet store, pharmacy, ice cream, jewelers, beauty salon, pools supply store, surf shop and realtor.

Marco Town Center Mall

This tropical old Florida style mall offers many great stores and restaurants and is the largest open air mall on Marco. It has entrances on Bald Eagle Drive, North Collier Blvd and East Elkcam Circle. Shops include ladies', men's and children's clothing from beachwear to up-market, swimwear, shoes, health food and grocery stores, specialty stores such as a gallery, home goods and accessories and a variety of restaurants.

The courtyard at Marco Walk is the center of night-time activity on the island. Five separate, and very different restaurants, offer indoor and pretty outdoor seating in the central courtyard There's also a movie theater (where you can enjoy anything from a beer to a full meal while watching the film), and several clothing stores as well as optical, vintage home goods and crafts, spa, hair and nail services, ice cream and real estate as well as a gelato and gourmet chocolate store.

This pretty Key West style area offers an award winning fish restaurant, gift shops, ladies' clothing, fresh fish shop, beauty salon, realty, a neighborhood bar and several art galleries. It is located on Royal Palm Drive at the northern most tip of the island.

Shops of Marco

Ladies' clothing, post office and gifts stores, beauty salon, dollar store and several restaurants join the island's largest grocery store in this large shopping mall.

Located 6 miles from Marco Island at 6060 Collier Blvd, Naples, FL 34114. Open daily 239.963.6666 6060 Collier Blvd., Naples, FL 34114

Over 140 top designer and brand name outlet stores and a wide variety of restaurants. Exit 123 off i75 on Corkscrew Road. (45 minutes from Marco). 239.948.3766

Wildlife

Eco tours and adventuresare, of course, the best way to see the amazing wildlife that surrounds Marco

Island, but just strolling on the beach you're likely to see dolphin fishing and playing just offshore, ospreys and brown pelicans diving for fish and a huge variety of shore birds feeding, and resting on the sands. If you're here in spring and summer you'll see the yellow warning tape around sea turtles nests which are dispersed along the beach and if you walk to the northern-most portion of the beach to the Tigertail area you'll likely see fiddler crabs in the vegetation at the back of the beach. Many different varieties of birds (some of them endangered) nest on the spit of land between the lagoon at Tigertail and the gulf and the area is sometimes closed to the public in the spring and summer to protect them.

Our many miles of canals are home to many species of fish and also endangered manatees. If you look carefully you may see their snouts or tails break the surface of the water as they come up for air, or the tell tail "footprint" left in the water as they submerge. Incidentally the water in the canals may look dirty but it is in fact just stained by tannin which comes from the mangrove trees - it is actually comparatively clean and unpolluted. If you're lucky you may also see ospreys diving in the canals and returning to their tree top nests with wriggling fish in their talons and perhaps even tarpon gulping air on the surface of the water.

Going a little further afield towards the Everglades you are almost certain to see wild alligators sunning themselves along the banks of the canals which run parallel to US 41. Although their numbers have increased enormously in recent years, they are still seen as an endangered species. This is due in part to the fact that SW Florida is also home to a small amount of salt water crocodiles (there is a small group of them near Marco airport just off the island) which are very rare and not easily distinguished from alligators - to ensure that no crocodiles are mistaken for alligators and killed, the alligators continue to be protected.

The Everglades

Coming to Marco Island and not visiting the Everglades is like going to Africa and not going on Safari... a trip into the Everglades is something you just can't miss! So here are some suggestions of where to go and what to do....

Take San Marco Road (SR 92) off the island past Goodland (a quaint little fishing village which is well worth a visit on another day as it has some great restaurants, an interesting clothing and jewelry store, as well as a whole lot of character).

Take a right when you reach US41 (The Tamiami Trail) and continue east a couple of miles until see a new parking lot on your right for the 10,000 Islands Wildlife Reserve. You can park here and take an easy walk down a track which takes you away from the road and into unspoiled grasslands and an easy to climb observation tower. In rainy season there's lots of water to reflect the puffy white clouds floating in the wide blue sky. It's incredibly peaceful, the landscape is just beautiful and you're likely to see lots of birds and wonderful butterflies. But do watch out for alligators as we've seen many of them there, as well as river otters.

Getting back on the road your next stop will be Port of the Islands, a little community which includes a hotel, a marina with boat launching facilities and some great eco tour and fishing captains. The majestic Faka Union canal leads from the marina out to the Gulf of Mexico and in winter it's home to hundreds of endangered manatee who congregate in its warm protected waters. You're also likely to see lots of alligators, waterbirds and the fishing here is great too.

If you'd like to get out on the water we recommend Capt. Barry, who offers 1½ hour private manatee tours (call 239-642-8818) and backwater fishing (239-389-0602),

Now for a little exercise.... Just a little further along US41 you'll see a sign for Fakahatchee Strand State Preserve, Big Cypress Bend Boardwalk, where the

2,000 ft long boardwalk provides an opportunity to experience the wonders of a rare ancient cypress forest. You'll walk close by an American Bald Eagle's nest, through amazing vegetation to a large and very beautiful pond which is usually alive with birds as well as adult and baby alligators. This boardwalk was badly damaged by Hurricane Irma but re-opened to the public in early November and is still very beautiful. But remember this is the Everglades and bug spray and long sleeved cotton clothing is a great idea.

The excitement of an airboat ride awaits you as you make your way further east on US 41. There's nothing quite like the thrill of speeding through the shallow waters of the Everglades as alligators slip calmly into the sparkling water and herons, egrets, and maybe even woodstorks, white pelicans and Roseate spoonbills, take flight as they hear you approach. We recommend Jungle Erv's (1-877-695-2820), which you'll find on US41 just before entering Everglades City. They have an on site store where you can get a cold drink, use the rest room and maybe buy a souvenir or two and every airboat tour comes with access to their riverside boardwalk (which you'll find if you take a right just before going over the bridge into Everglades City), with an exotic bird exhibit, an alligator exhibit and show and maybe even the chance, if you're brave enough, to hold an alligator.

Everglades City is getting into the heart of old Florida. Once planned to be the capital of Collier County, Everglades City boasts wide tree lined avenues and surprisingly elaborate buildings like the City Hall and Rod and Gun Club. It was also badly damaged with devasting flooding, by Hurricane Irma, but it is certainly still very much worth a visit.

Break for lunch at Triad Seafood Cafe & Market (239-695-2262) for some all you can eat stone crabs. They are open 7 days in season (but closed for much of the summer) and are famous for their "All you can Eat" Stone Crab dinners and their fabulous homemade key lime pie.

The Museum of the Everglades, close to the city's enormous central traffic circle, offers a fascinating insight into the area's history as does the Smallwood Store and Museum, an old, amazingly well preserved, Indian trading post at the end of a scenic ten minute drive down a causeway to the shell island of Chokoloskee.

While you're in Chokoloskee don't forget to stop by JT's Gallery (239-695-2630) - which features local art, crafts and books about the area, and maybe book a tour with Everglades Area Tours 239-204-5344. Their many guided tours, which include boat assisted guided kayak tours, mangrove tunnel kayak tours, birding, photography, walking and fishing tours, offer a fantastic way to get up close and personal with the birds and animals that call this endangered environment home.

On your way back from Chokoloskee stop by the visitor center at The Everglades National Park to learn more about the park, which is one of the largest in the US and is particularly valued for its biological diversity with, over 300 kinds of birds and dozens of endangered species.

Now, if you really want to see alligators in their natural environment return to US41 and head east to the HP Williams Boardwalk. It will take you about ten minutes and on the way look out for the smallest post office in the entire United States.

The short boardwalk at HP Williams is a wonderful place to spot alligators as they sun themselves on the river bank or glide ominously through the dark but sparkling water. After your walk, if you don't mind getting your car a little dirty, take a drive up the dirt road which follows the path of the river - it can get a little overgrown but you're likely to see a lot more alligators at really close quarters there - but be careful and remember they can run faster than you over short distances!

Of course just driving through the Everglades is an experience in itself so your journey home will be a joy - it's not spectacular scenery but it is incredibly beautiful, especially in the evening when the light is soft and the birds are active. Cloud formations out there can be enormous and ever-changing and an Everglades sunset has to be one of the most serenely beautiful things you can ever experience.

Marco Island Shopping

Bald Eagle Drive

CRITTER CAFE - this pet resort and spa offers a full range of holistic, all natural pet foods, organicbakery treats and unique gifts for pets as well as 5-star doggie boarding, daycare and a full service grooming salon. www.crittercafemarcoisland.com 810 Bald Eagle Drive. 239.389.8488.

ISLAND BIKE SHOP & SCOOTERTOWN - full service bicycle sales and repairs www.islandbikeshops.com. 1095 Bald Eagle Dr, 239.394.8400

ISLAND COASTAL OUTFITTERS - this recently beautifully remodeled store offers one of the largest selections of apparel, shoes and accessories, for all the family, available on the island. Based in Rose Marina, it also has a wide selection of Bote paddle boards and other fine coastal equipment, including fishing tackle and boating supplies. The marina also offers boat rentals, gas and diesel sales for boats and is home to many of Marco's finest fishing charters and boat tours. www.IslandCoastal.com or www.rose marina.com. 951 Bald Eagle Drive, 239.394.2502

Collier Blvd
JEWELRY BY LAURA - for the last 25 years this jewelry store, which is located in the lobby of the JW Marriott Hotel, has offered something for everyone. No matter what your budget you're sure to find something perfect from their large selection of Sterling silver, fashion jewelry and14/18 kt gold and diamond jewelry. 239.389.0190

MAKE A MEMORY - specializing in gift baskets and bonded fruit shipping this well stocked store also offers a great selection of unique gifts, Florida products, bath and body products and Gourmet Chocolates. www.makeamemory.com. 277 N Collier Blvd. 239.642.3600 or 800.524.4144   Please note Make a Memory will be relocating to 567 E. Elkcam Circle (opposite the main post office and next door to Hoot's) in late March.

OMG THAT'S CHIC - formerly located in Marco Town Center Mall, this store is bound to inject a little whimsy into your life with an eclectic collection of very reasonably priced ladies' clothing which is designed to please all tastes and to fit all shapes and sizes. And when it comes to accessories there's plenty of bling to make your outfits sing... sparkle abounds and there's also a great selection of one of a kind jewelry. www.omgthatschic.com. 287 N Collier Blvd.
239.970.2102

SUNSATIONS - this large store offers everything you could need for the perfect beach vacation including brand named clothing, swimwear, shoes and sunglasses for all the family as well as kids' toys, pool toys, beach chairs and more.   671 S Collier Blvd (opposite Charter Club). 239.393.0555

SUNSHINE BOOKSELLERS - with two locations on Collier Blvd, these well stocked stores offer the best in books for vacation reading as well as newspapers, greeting cards and gifts. The north store also offers mailboxes, UPS and FedEx Shipping and the south store incorporates a full service US Post Office. www.sunshinebooksellers.com. 1000, N Collier Blvd #14. 239.394.5343 and 677 S Collier Blvd.
239.393.0353

THE PRESSED OLIVE - This brand new store is Marco's new source for more than 22 different fused and infused extra virgin olive oils and 22 flavors of premium balsamic vinegars. There's also a great selection of cookwear, kitchen gadgets and serving dishes as well as a unique range of gourmet foods, like freeze dried soups, unusual glazes and pasta/BBQ sauces as well as locally made products like Amelia Island toffee, Marco Island Honey Company honey and lots more. www.ThePressedOliveStore.com 919 North Collier Blvd., in Flagship Harbor Plaza, between Verizon and Michelbob's. 239.970.5231

The Esplanade
An up-market Italian style retail and dining center overlooking the marina on beautiful Smokehouse Bay. With its fountains, waterfront restaurants, large courtyard with open air bar, and ice cream shops, this is a great place to wander around and visit the galleries and stores www.esplanadeshoppes.com

BUTTERFLY BEACH - a colorful, ever-evolving specialty clothing store offering unique, affordable and fun apparel, swimwear, accessories and shoes. With handpicked name brands which reflect the latest trends in the fashion world you're sure to find something for everyone in the family.

www.butterflybeachclothing.com. 760 N. Collier Blvd, Unit 103 in the Esplanade. 239.394.0837

C'EST LA VIE - a great little store offers cutting edge ladies' clothing and accessories, which are guaranteed to get you noticed!   740 N Collier Blvd., Unit 108. 239.970.2438

YARA'S SHOE BOUTIQUE - This delightful, relatively new, store offers a wide ranging collection of shoes and accessories which is carefully selected to appeal to all ages... from stylish comfort shoes to high fashion pumps there's something for all tastes. Follow Yara's Shoe Boutique on Twitter, Instagram and Facebook. 760 North Collier Blvd., #102 in the Esplanade. 239.394.2323

Goodland
This quaint old fishing village, just minutes from Marco Island, boasts several great waterfront restaurants and offers a rare taste of Old Florida.

FIA'S ISLAND BOUTIQUE - has a great new look post Hurricane Irma. Reflecting Goodland's eclectic nature, the fishing village's only retail store offers a unique blend of easy to wear island style clothing, fashion jewelry and gifts. Located right next to Stan's Idle Hour Restaurant, Fia's Island Boutique presents a fashion show during Stan's famous Sunday concerts and offers a great selection of novelty wear and Stan's memorabilia - essential accoutrements for the full Stan's Sunday experience. Open Tuesday - Sunday 11am-6pm.   www.fiasislandwoman.com. 239.642.6116.

Marco Town Center Mall
Marco's largest shopping center, this spacious tropical mall has 30 great restaurants and stores, including Publix. It offers a huge variety of merchandise including beach, casual and formal wear, shoes, jewelry, health foods a gallery and is also home to Marco's active community theatre, The Marco Players.   Located on the South east corner of the intersection of Collier Blvd

and Bald Eagle Drive, it has entrances on Bald Eagle, Collier Blvd and East Elkcam Circle.

BEACHWORKS - Since Terri Knapp bought this long established store a few years ago she has brought a great new energy to it. With quality brand name apparel for all the family such as Fresh Produce, Big Hed, Pete Huntinton and Kahala and a great selection of men's and ladies' shoes they also offer luxurious beach towels and beach puffs, local interest books for adults and children and island gifts. They also stock Bug-N-Burn, a wonderfully soothing anti-itch and sunburn cream. www.beachworksonline.com 239.642.7777

BLUE MANGROVE GALLERY - this lively gallery, which changed hands last summer, offers a wonderful selection of tropical art and photography, Florida designed accent furniture, artisan jewelry and handcrafted gifts to please all tastes. You'll find an enticing children's section, handbags and textiles, hand blown glass and pottery as well as a full selection of

Key West Aloe and Naples Soap Company products and Marco Island Candle Company candles. Their Dune Jewelry incorporates Marco Island authentic sand and they have a great selection of Lizzy James jewelry, hand made in the USA. Fun, colorful and inspiring - a favorite among the locals, visitors and a great destination stop! www.bluemangrovegallery.com. 239.393.2405.

MARGARITAVILLE ISLAND RESERVE - this brand new store offers a nice variety of casual men's clothing from Jimmy Buffet's popular clothing range as well as men's hats, shoes and LandShark sunglasses. It is owned and run by the ladies from Beachworks (see above) so we know it's going to be good! 239.970.0708 / 239.970.0809

ISLAND TIME - for a great selection of brand name casual apparel, shoes, and Marco embroidered wear for the whole family, at the best prices, visit Island Time. Also featuring Marco's largest selection of crocs for men, women and children as well as a great selection of cool summer dresses and T-shirts perfect for the island's hot summer climate. 239.970.2277

MARCO CRAFT AND SHELL CO - has relocated to Marco Walk with a new name.... SHORE GOODS.

SANDPIPER CLOTHIERS - quality clothing, shoes and

accessories from famous brand names such as Lilly Pulitzer, Vineyard Vines and Tori Richard attract a wide range of customers (men, women and children) to this long established family run Marco Island store, which also has sister branches in Naples and Key Largo. Check out their newly expanded children's department. www.sandpiperclothiers.com. 239.642.6691

THE UPS STORE - avoid airport hassles by getting your excess luggage packed and shipped home ahead of time by the UPS store. They also offer a huge selection of packing supplies, in-store computer rental, high speed internet, copying, notary services and mail boxes. 239.642.0011

YOUR ISLAND HOME - there's no need to leave the island to find a great selection of high quality, yet reasonably priced, home decor and gift items - just visit Your Island Home in their new, larger location in suite #420! From luxurious bamboo linens, sumptuous towels and decorative pillows to colorful serving pieces, stemwear, lamps, photo frames and artwork, this store offers a remarkably wide choice of tropically themed items including locally hand painted holiday decorations and Marco Cat gifts.

www.yourislandhome.com 239.642.7366

Marco Walk Plaza
The entertainment and dining center of the island. Catch a newly released movie, or dine at one of the five fabulous restaurants which offer indoor seating as well as outdoor in the pretty central courtyard with its fountains and lively buzz. www.marcowalkplaza.com. 599 South Collier Blvd, across from the Hilton.

BEACH DAISY - One of Marco's most exciting clothing and accessory boutiques, specializing in effortless lifestyle clothing, jewelry, shoes and accessories with an emphasis on USA made lines. . www.beachdaisy.net. 239.394.0169

OPTICAL BOUTIQUE - celebrating 23 years on Marco Island this great little boutique offers prescription and non-prescription designer eyewear featuring Tom Ford, Versace, Bobbi Brown, Caviar/Cazal, Diva, Lafont, Maui Jim, Ray-Ban Stella McCartney and more. 239.642.4776 See our feature in our Winter 2013 edition e-magazine

SHORE GOODS - this fascinating store, which relocated from Marco Town Center Mall and changed its name in early summer 2018, has a huge selection of vintage home accents and locally made handcrafted gifts. It will inspire you to get crafty and take advantage of their great selection of art supplies, specimen shells, Marco Island memory book and jewelry supplies. www.shoregoods.store. 239.394.7020

Shops of Marco
One of Marco's longest established shopping centers, the Shops of Marco offers a great variety of stores

including the island's largest Publix, a liquor store, dollar store and several restaurants. Located at the south east corner of the intersection of San Marco Road and S Barfield Drive.

KATHEIN JEWELERS OF MARCO - formerly Golden Gate Jewelers of Marco - this beautifully appointed store now sports the family name and offers a huge selection of fine jewelry and interesting art work. Family owned and operated, they perform all repairs, custom design work and appraisals in house. The Kathein family have had a fine jewelry store in Fort Lauderdale for over 30 years and, having fallen in love with Marco some years ago, they fulfilled a dream when they opened their second location here on Marco in 2014. www.ggjmarco.com. 239.259.8937 See article in our Season 2016 edition

KEEP IN TOUCH - this busy store has a wide selection of gifts, greeting cards, stationery, candles and souvenirs and Life is Good clothing. They also offer Marco Island products like cookies, honey and candles as well as fruit shipping, packing, boxes and shipping supplies, computer stations with high speed internet as well as printing, fax and notary services. And, best of all, their US Post Office contract postal unit, now with two stations, is open whenever the shop is. www.keepintouchstore.com 239.393.6300

TONGA'S DESIGNS - in addition to a great collection of fine ladies fashions, including beach, resort and cruise wear, this unique store also offers a wide selection of formal wear, including 'Mother-of-the-Bride", as well as accessories, jewelry and alterations. 239.642-8750

SALON AND SPA BOTANICA - Committed to both the world of beauty and the world's environment, this salon and spa carries an extensive range of organic Aveda beauty products for use in the salon and to take home. www.salonandspabotanica.com. 239.394.6633

The Shops at Olde Marco
This colorful key West style shopping area is located in a cobbled courtyard behind Café de Marco and boasts several art galleries, stores, a beauty salon, gelato store

and restaurants. Take Bald Eagle as far north as you can go and bear to the left onto Royal Palm Drive). www.CollectionOnMarco.com

BIJOUX - this sophisticated, little boutique aims to offer something different from the other "beachy" Marco Island stores. So if you're looking for something a little out of the ordinary stop by and take a look at its selection of gifts, home goods, jewelry, body care products, baby clothes and specialty clothing. 239.970.6099.

LOCAL COLOR ART GALLERY - this artist owned gallery located on the mezzanine above the shops features the work of many local artists. There's lots to see including textiles, sculpture, oils, jewelry, water colors, photography, fiber art, children's books and custom framing. www.malendatrick.com/localcolor. 239.394.2787 or cell 615.292.9110

South Heathwood Drive
MARCO ISLAND HISTORICAL SOCIETY GIFT SHOP - When you shop at this store you will not only have the

choice of a mix of work by local artists and artisans, including paintings and reproductions of Calusa masks, but there's also a wide selection of books, plush toys and unique jewelry. And, most important of all, you will also be contributing to the development and upkeep of this important museum which opens a window onto the fascinating past of Marco Island. Open 10am-3pm Tuesday to Saturday. 180 S Heathwood Drive. 239.389. 6447.. www.themihs.org

Winterberry Drive
MARCO ISLAND CENTER FOR THE ARTS GIFT SHOP - Offers an opportunity to purchase all kinds of items made by local artists and to help support the local artistic community. From custom made charms (made by Kathein Jewelers of Marco), oil and watercolor paintings to hand made pottery, jewelry, silks and soaps, there's a great selection at very reasonable prices. 239.394.4221, 1010 Winterberry Drive www.marcoislandart.org

General

MARCO ISLAND FARMERS' MARKET - this seasonal weekly open air market offers fresh fruits, garden vegetables, herbs, fresh flowers, seafood, baked goods, honey, sauces, kettle popcorn, chocolates, fresh flowers, soaps, exotic jewelry and works from local artists. Every Wednesday 7:30am-1pm from thru April 24th 2019. Veterans' Community Park, 901 Park Avenue. For more details call 239.642.0575 or visit www.cityofmarcoisland.com

MARCO ISLAND CANDLE COMPANY - This island based company incorporates the highest quality waxes and highest quality fragrance oils for a perfect candle that doesn't sacrifice your health or home. Each candle is thoughtfully crafted in small batches, handmade locally with love. Every candle provides a $1 donation to a local charity here on the Island. Marco Island Candle Company candles are available at several island stores and it has also recently open its own retail space at 9 Front Street and is now offering "Candles in the

Kitchen" - candle making parties in your own home. 507.206.7878

JO-ANN SANBORN - specializing in the art of the Everglades local artist Jo-Ann Sanborn has closed Sunshine Gallery at the Esplanade but you can still see her work on her Facebook page and site www.joannsanborn.com. 239.404.9179

ROOKERY BAY NATURE STORE - You will find an assortment of wonderful gifts for the family or maybe a souvenir for yourself... books, clothes, stuffed animals, souvenirs and other gifts that embody the unique estuarine environment in Southwest Florida. Every purchase from The Rookery Bay Nature Store supports the Friends of Rookery Bay and its mission to provide resources for Rookery Bay Research Reserve's education, research and stewardship programs. Open Monday–Saturday 9.00am to 4.00pm. 300 Tower Road, Naples. www.RookeryBay.org 239.530.5940

Activities

Fishing

Big fish, tough fighting fish and great edible fish....
Marco Island has it all and is quite possibly one of THE
best places to find varied fishing all year round. Being
the northern-most of the 10,000 Islands, surrounded
by natural preserves and bordering the Gulf of Mexico,
Marco is ideally situated to offer many different kinds
of world class fishing. You'll find below a description of
the different opportunities available here and what
you can expect from each if you go out on a fishing
charter. I would recommend that you narrow down
what you are looking for and what suits your party
best. The list below will help you decide which of our
highly experienced Charter Captains will be just right
for you.

Family Fishing
If you want to take the family out for some fun and you
haven't been fishing in Southwest Florida before, or
you just aren't a die-hard, then nearshore or backwater
could be your best bet. Depending on the time of year

you will have a shot at snapper, sheepshead, snook, redfish, grouper, tarpon, trout, blackdrum, pompano and tripletail. When the water warms in the summer there are also numerous species of shark to add to the mix, including blacktip, hammerhead, bonnethead and bull. You won't have to travel far and you will get plenty of fishing on a half day trip. Some of the guides that specialize in nearshore and backwater fishing will also mix a trip with shelling and birdwatching to please the non-fishermen (or women!) in your party. Talk to the captain about your party's particular needs and ask what he suggests targeting the day of your charter... you will be delighted with the time you spend.

Backwater for the More Experienced Angler
If you take your fishing seriously, then you should take a day out with any of our amazing backwater guides in the 10.000 islands and Everglades National Park - you're sure to be happy that you did. You can use a fly or spinning rod depending on your level of expertise and the captain will probably target snook, redfish,

snapper or the most fantastic of all local gamefish, the tarpon. Tarpon in the backwaters or along the beaches can range in size from 3 to 6 feet and although they don't hit the bait hard, you'll know you're in for the fight of your life when they start that run and make their first leap clear of the water!!

Of course you could also end up with a shark, grouper, jack or ladyfish - but it will be a fun day casting up against the mangroves hardly seeing another person and bringing that monster snook, tarpon or shark to the boat. You will not believe how big the fish are in these skinny waters.

Offshore for the Big Boys (Fish and Guys!)
A day (or half day if you have to limit your excitement!) of offshore fishing on a number of the wrecks, artificial reefs or fish havens will keep everybody quiet on the trip back to the marina! Some species you're likely to find, depending on the time of year, are Goliath grouper, barracuda, tripletail, sheepshead, snapper, cobia, amberjack, mackerel, shark and grouper and

they always make for fishing fun. There are many charter captains, with larger boats, specializing in offshore fishing and they will definitely bend your rod! Again the list below will help you decide which captain is best for you.

Going it Alone
Marco's certainly a great place to fish whether you're a novice, a die-hard or just fancy a novel workout. If you choose to go with a charter captain, you will only need to take food, drink and sunscreen for your trip. However, if you want to try from land then either the beaches (not near designated swimming areas of course) or the areas around the two bridges linking Marco to the mainland, are always worth a try. The waterway behind your rental home is likely to have mangrove snapper, sheepshead, jack, snook, redfish and catfish around the dock or swimming by. If your waterway is closer to the Gulf you may be fortunate to find some of the smaller tarpon cruising up and down. It's always a surprise (and great fun) to see a three foot

tarpon explode from the water in one of our waterways.

Remember to check that the fish you've caught are legal sized and in season before you keep them and that you may be required to have a valid fishing license - you can pick up information on this at a local marina. Also don't forget that most

of the local restaurants will be happy to cook your fresh catch for you and prepare it to your liking, as long as you have cleaned it first!

Charter Captains We Recommend:

Capt Barry
Backwater & Everglades National Park fishing with tournament champion Capt Barry. Also offering two hour "Teach Your Kids to Fish" fishing charters. 239-389-0602

DREAMLANDER TOURS -Four hour private half day backwater fishing tours with experienced USCG captains. 239.331.3775

Fins-N-Grins
Backwater & nearshore charter fishing, sightseeing, shelling and eco-tours leaving from Calusa Island Marina, Goodland. Call Capt Michael Van Jones at 239-784-2442

FLORIDA ADVENTURES AND RENTALS - Offering backwater and offshore fishing charters as well as kayak and paddleboard fishing. 239.348.5551

Mangrove Maniacs
Backwater and kayak fishing with Capt Drew Naeckel, owner operator with over 21 years local experience. Spinning and fly fishing. 239-777-5707

Reel Thrills Fishing Charters
Offshore and inshore fishing for the novice or experienced angler with Captain Erix Rodriguez. His 35 years experience fishing Southwest Florida guarantees you a great time on the water. Stable, new 29ft Parker with extremely quiet Yamaha engines. Lots of room for up to 6 people to fish. Clean enclosed restroom

onboard.   www.reelthrillsfishingcharters.com.

239.825.4611

Six Chuter Charters

You're guaranteed to catch fish on this four boat fleet located at Rose Marco River Marina. Backwater, nearshore & offshore fishing with combo trips including shelling and sightseeing for the whole family. 239-389-1575

Sunshine Tours

Backcountry, nearshore and offshore fishing with private and shared charters. With five charter boats and eight captains, Sunshine Tours has the waterfront covered. Their latest addition is a 36ft Yellowfin with triple 300 hp engines capable of cruising at 50 mph. Celebrating nearly 35 years on Marco. 239-642-5415

Wild Thing Charters

Capt Randy Hamlton will take you offshore and make your rod sing on his custom 30' cagbin boat with rest room. 239-821-7054

On The Water Eco Adventures

As a visitor there are many ways to explore the balmy waters around Marco Island and to see the wonderful aquatic wildlife and birds which surround us. You can either go it alone and **rent** a boat, kayak or jetski

(see below for details) or take one of the many water tours which are available in the area.

Boat Rentals

DOLPHIN COVE MARINA - The closest marina boat rental to top destinations including Keewaydin Island and Coconut Island, (just 5 minutes of slow speed zone and then you're off!) and, unlike other marinas, at Dolphin Cove Marina there are little to no restrictions on where you can/cannot go and no rental advertisement or phone numbers on the boats. Rent a fishing boat and head offshore or a 20-23ft Hurricane deck boat or a 22-25ft pontoon boat for cruising and fishing in the bays and backwaters. They will even deliver to the dock behind your rental home or condo for an extra $50 to drop off and $50 to pick up. Half day, full day and weekly rentals at very reasonable rates. 1135 Bald Eagle Drive. Map1 (2C) 239.289.8654

ROSE MARINA - Pontoon, center console, and deck boat rentals as well as bait & tackle, ship's store, full service boatyard, gas and diesel and wet/dry storage. 951 Bald Eagle Drive 239-394-2502

Kayak, & Paddleboard Rentals

DOLPHIN COVE MARINA - Start your 1 or 2 person kayak or paddleboard rental at Caxambas Park and explore the quiet backwaters of the 10,000 islands at your own pace. Or, choose to have it delivered to your rental home or condo on Marco or Capri for an additional $10. Half day, full day rental or more. 239.289.8654

FLORIDA ADVENTURES AND RENTALS - Single and tandem kayaks available. Also offering free delivery and pick up of half and full day kayak and paddleboard rentals on Marco, Goodland and Isles of Capri. Launch from Capri Paddlecraft Park or Caxambas Park. 239.348.5551

KOOL CAT SUP RENTALS Craig Cat tour operator Kool Cat has ventured into SUP rentals. Departing from Shell Road, you will be shown how to safely operate the board and where to explore the calm waters of Rookery Bay to maximize the adventure. Coolers are available for your drinks and snacks. All rentals are two hours. 239.888.1069

NAPLES SALTWATER ADVENTURES - Kayak and paddle board rentals from Capri Fish House in Isles of Capri. 239.228.9383

PADDLE MARCO - Single and double kayaks and paddleboards for rent by the hour, day or week at affordable prices. Paddle Marco will provide laminated maps and directions to nearby uninhabited barrier islands and sand bars for amazing shelling. Free delivery and pickup to any boat launch or home on Marco Island, Goodland or Isles of Capri. Paddle Marco even pay the launch fees at the parks. Rentals include life jackets, maps, dry bags and cellphone containers. 239 777.5423

Wave Runner Rentals

DOLPHIN COVE MARINA ½ day, full day and weekly jet ski rentals at very reasonable rates, from the closest marina to top destinations including Keewaydin Island and Coconut Island, (just 5 minutes of slow speed zone and then you're off!). 1135 Bald Eagle Drive. 239.289.8654

MARCO ISLAND JET SKI TOURS & RENTALS - Arrange free pick up at your hotel or Marco Island home. Rentals leave daily from Caxambas Park. 239.888.2488

MARCO ISLAND WATERSPORTS Waverunner rentals from the beach outside the hotels. Also offering guided waverunner tours. Leaving from the beach huts at the Marco Island Marriott Resort (642-2359) or the Hilton Beach Resort Map 1 (7B & 8B) (642-3377) Call 239.389.4FUN

Guided Tours On the Water

When it comes to tours there's a really wide choice.... private small motor or sail boat tours, large party motor boat tours, airboat tours, guided paddle board tours, guided kayak tours and, last but not least, guided waverunner tours into the 10,000 Islands. To help you decide which option is right for you see our suggestions below:

Airboat Tours
JUNGLE ERV'S AIRBOAT TOURS - Small airboat tours in the heart of the Everglades. Choose from several different tours which all include a stroll along the newly upgraded boardwalk bordering the Barron River to manatee point where manatees are sighted daily. Enjoy the alligator and exotic bird exhibits and finish with an alligator show and maybe the chance to hold an alligator. 804 Collier Avenue, Everglades City. 877.695.2820

Craigcat Tours
BACKWATER ADVENTURE - Leaving from behind the Little Bar restaurant in Goodland, after a 15 minute brief on how to drive the boats, you're underway and it's off on a great boating experience. Winding through

the mangroves around the 10,000 islands on the water is as beautiful as it gets. Narrow mangrove tunnels give you a great driving experience, but following behind your guide (either Captain Doug or his son in law, Captain Conner) there is no danger of getting lost. About midway through the 2½ hour trip, there is a stop on a barrier island for shelling and swimming. The entire trip will cover 30 to 40 miles of the most beautiful waterways around Marco and the Everglades. As a courtesy, and at no extra charge, your guide will take pictures and email them to you after your adventure. When you return, why not have lunch or dinner at the Little Bar, one of our favorite local restaurants. Minimum driver age is 18 years and the minimum passenger age is 5 years. 239-877-4531

KOOLCAT ECO TOURS - KoolCat Eco Tours operate four CraigCats that leave from either the boat ramp on SR951 or Goodland Boat Park depending upon the tides. Their 3 hour tours combine open water excitement and slow passages through the mangroves as you look for shorebirds, dolphin and manatees. Their tour guides, Derek and Jason, stay in touch using walkie talkies and let you know when to look for dolphins, manatees and other interesting wildlife along the route. They know the area well and, as they say, will make your trip "as memorable as the sunsets in the Gulf of Mexico". All of the photos taken on the tour will be shared with customers by email later the same day. Minimum driver age is 18 and the minimum passenger age is 5 years. 239.888.1069

MARCO ISLAND ECO TOURS - operates two and a half hour guided CraigCat tours leaving from Goodland Boat Park and passing through some of the 10,000 Islands. Reaching speeds of up to 30 mph in the open water, you will slow down to watch any of the wildlife you encounter along the way and when going through the mangroves. Tour guide and owner Captain Tony Isse, will take you within arm's reach of dolphins as you explore the bays and creeks of the 10,000 Islands where you're likely to encounter osprey, manatees and lots of shorebirds. Although their schedule is based on tides, they usually stop off at Whitehorse Key or Gullivan Key, both deserted barrier islands, for a short time. Although only recently starting up CraigCat tours, Tony has over 25 years of experience in these waters and will provide you with an experience you'll probably want to repeat again and again! Minimum driver age is 19 years and minimum passenger age is 10 years. 239.394.1455

Kayak & Paddle Board Tours

EVERGLADES AREA TOURS - A mother boat takes you deep into the Everglades National Park where you'll start your guided kayak and/or fishing adventure. Also offering extended camping and specialty photography trips and mangrove tunnel kayak eco tours deep in the Everglades - the quiet alternative to airboats! 239-204-5382

FLORIDA ADVENTURES AND RENTALS - 2-hour Kayak tours on the relaxing calm waters of Rookery Bay. Local, professional guides (Florida Master Naturalists) take you through mangrove mazes and tunnels where you can discover some of South Florida's most popular wildlife. Whether you're a beginner or an advanced kayaker, you will enjoy every minute! Tours leave daily from the Isles of Capri Paddlecraft Park just minutes from Marco Island. Single and tandem kayaks and paddleboards available. 239.348.5551

MANGROVE MANIACS - Fully customizable Florida Master Naturalist-led boat and kayak eco tours, shelling and sunset excursions with Capt Drew Naeckel. This real Florida experience will be the highlight of your stay. 239-777-5707

MARCO ISLAND BOAT TOURS - Boat assisted kayak eco tours with formally trained Florida Master Naturalists, environmental educators and full-time outdoor leaders. 239.674-0649

NAPLES SALTWATER ADVENTURES - Kayak and paddle board rentals and tours, fishing charters and kayak fishing tours from Capri Fish House in Isles of Capri. 239.228.9383

PADDLE MARCO - Guided kayak eco-tours launched from Capri Paddlecraft Park through amazing mangrove tunnels and mudflats, while looking for incredible wildlife including dolphins, manatees and sea stars. Single and double kayaks and paddleboards for rent by the hour, day or week at affordable prices. Free delivery and pickup to any boat launch or home on Marco Island, Goodland or Isles of Capri. Paddle Marco even pay the launch fees at the parks. Rentals include life jackets, maps, dry bags and cellphone containers. 239 777.5423

ROOKERY BAY - Experience the nature of Rookery Bay Research Reserve up-close and personal on one of their naturalist-guided kayak tours. All tours provide a chance to see a diversity of native wildlife and offer a comfortable platform for photography. Visit for dates, times and themes. 239.530.5940

Motor Boat Eco Tours

BACKWATER ADVENTURE - offers a 3 hour luxury champagne eco tour on their 24 foot pontoon boat. Leaving from the Little Bar on Goodland their tours are limited to a maximum of six passengers. This tour circumnavigates the islands of Marco and Goodland, visiting the dome home at Cape Romano and stopping off for some shelling, weather permitting. The tour can be adjusted to suit your needs, with complimentary bubbly and tasty snacks served on-board. Then, when you return, you'll be ready to enjoy lunch or dinner at one of our favorite local restaurants, the Little Bar - you won't have far to walk! 239-877.4531

BANYAN CHARTERS - Half day and full day private boat tours for 6 including shelling and sightseeing, dolphin and sunset tours. Per person 2 hour sunset tours available also. Owner Captain Austin has been boating on Marco and surrounding waters for over 30 years and wants you to have a day of rest and relaxation at sea. Banyan Charters boat is a 2015 Starcraft SCX250 and can comfortably seat 13 passengers, although tours are limited to just 6. So rest assured that you will have plenty of room to stretch out and relax while on the water. They provide two coolers, with water and ice and they also have a fresh water wash down. Complimentary beach chairs and umbrellas are provided on all tours. Leaving from Caxambas Park. 239.595.3269

CALUSA SPIRIT by Marco Island Watersports - everyone will love this unforgettable 2½ hour dolphin watch/shelling trip aboard this spacious and well shaded 49 passenger, 45' catamaran with full restroom. Departs directly from the beach in fine weather or from Calusa Marina in Goodland when the Gulf is rough but the backwaters are calm. Enjoy views of playful dolphins in their natural habitat while learning about the local ecosystem of mangrove estuaries on your way to Cape Romano, where you will have about an hour to shell, explore, swim and admire the remains of the dome home just offshore. (239) 642-2359

DOC JIMMY'S CURE-ALL MARINE ADVENTURES - Satisfaction is guaranteed on these private or group sunset tours and 3 hour shelling excursions to Keewaydin and Cape Romano. Doc. Jimmy's is affiliated with popular waverunner tour Capt. Ron's Awesome Everglades Adventures and, with our coupon, if you book a jet ski tour with Capt. Ron's you will get $100 off per party of two or more on tours with Doc Jimmy's. Like Capt. Ron's, Doc Jimmy's has an underwater microphone so you can hear dolphins communicating with each other under water. 239.777.9975

DOLPHIN EXPLORER - 3 hour eco, photo expedition where you can participate in dolphin study with naturalist on 28 passenger power cat. Visit their booking cart at Rose Marco River Marina, 951 Bald Eagle Drive. Map1 (3C) 642-6899

DREAMLANDER TOURS - offer two and three hour dolphin and shelling tours either on a per person basis, or as a private tour. A licensed US Coast Guard Captain will guide you through the Ten Thousand Islands, showing you wildlife (focusing mainly on dolphins), vegetation and the famous Cape Romano Dome Home. Some tours also include stopping on a barrier island for a chance to collect some shells and explore on the beautiful white sand. 239.331.3775

EVERGLADES AREA TOURS - see wonderful wildlife and enjoy amazing shelling on these 2 hour naturalist led, power boat excursions. Explore the backwaters of the 10,000 Islands and the pristine Gulf beaches. Leaving from Calusa Island Marina in Goodland and Chokoloskee, Everglades City. Reservations required. 239-204-5382

FLORIDA ADVENTURES AND RENTALS - 3 hour shelling tours departing from Caxambas Park. See the Cape Romano dome home then stop on a secluded beach in search of shells that the Gulf coast is known for. This is a semi-private, or private boat tour with a maximum of 6 guests. These tours are very kid friendly with a bathroom, sink, comfortable seating and a ladder off the back of the boat for easy boarding. 239.348.5551

GREENWATER BOAT TOURS - take a boat tour through the bays and backwaters of the 10,000 islands showcasing nature's beauty and marine life. Stop by Cape Romano to see the historic dome home. Feel like you are on your own private island, relax and enjoy a picnic lunch. Walk the beaches to collect sea shells, sand dollars or take a swim in the Gulf. Call Captain Mike Green to schedule your personalized eco boat trip leaving from Caxambas Park. 239-290-8900

HEMINGWAY WATER SHUTTLE - Based at Rose Marina, Hemingway Water Shuttle operates a daily shuttle to Keewaydin Island on a 22 passenger pontoon boat. The trip takes around 30 minutes and you can add a beach chair rental for $10.   They also offer sunset tours and party and custom tours. 239.315.1136

ISLAND GYPSY EXCURSIONS - 3 hour historical/ecological and shelling tours, for up to 6 passengers, departing from Goodland Boat Park. USCG licensed captain/naturalist Nancy will explain the area's history as you meander through the mangrove islands. 239.450.2800

MANATEE SIGHTSEEING ADVENTURE - Personal 1½ hour eco-tour into a remote manatee hideout. Quality manatee visuals guaranteed. No see - no pay! Only 2-6 passengers on 13 passenger rated boats so there's no crowding and there's plenty of room for your manatee encounter. After a dynamite manatee visual, check out alligators, endangered birds and more manatees. See why nature lovers take this tour two or three times per year. Map3 (23Q). Call your new friends, Captains Barry and Carol 239-642-8818

MANATEE SUNSET TOURS - Captains Barry & Carol are well known for their manatee sightseeing tours leaving from Port of the Islands and they recently added "Manatees and Sunset" to their repertoire. Just a 15 minute drive from Marco, not only will you have the opportunity to see a fabulous Gulf sunset but probably get to see manatees too, 'cos Captain Barry knows where they hang out! Bring your own drinks to toast the sun as it dips below the horizon for another beautiful sunset. 239.642.8818

MANGROVE MANIACS - Fully customizable Florida Master Naturalist-led boat eco tours, shelling and sunset excursions with Capt Drew Naeckel. This real Florida experience will be the highlight of your stay. 239-777-5707

MARCO ISLAND BOAT TOURS - A division of Everglades Area Tours, offers two hour dolphin and shelling tours as well as half day family fun dolphin/shelling/beach/fishing trips. All guides are formally trained Florida Master Naturalists, environmental educators and full-time outdoor leaders. 239.674.0649

MARCO ISLAND WATERSPORTS - the Calusa Spirit, a spacious and well shaded 49 passengers, 45' catamaran with full rest room, offers amazing shelling on deserted beaches, sunset cruises and private adventures. Leaving from the beach at the Marco Island Marriott Resort, the Hilton Beach Resort or Calusa Marina in Goodland when the Gulf is rough but the backwaters are calm.   Map 1 (7B & 8B)   Call 239.389.4FUN

PARADISE COAST MARINE SERVICES - - Enjoy a custom, private charter aboard a meticulously maintained 25' center console, Hot Pursuit, which includes a full marine head. If you want to look for dolphins, owner/Captain Jamie will do it. Lunch in Goodland, Naples, or Everglades City? He can do that. If you are interested in shelling or bird watching, he'll take you to the hot spots. Or the private beach tour is a chance for you, your family, and friends to enjoy fun in the sun on an island that can only be accessed by boat. 954.361.4131

ROOKERY BAY - Experience the nature of Rookery Bay Research Reserve up-close and personal on one of their naturalist-guided boat tours. The relaxed pace and emphasis on learning is designed to help visitors develop a true sense of place and a deeper connection to this unique coastal wilderness. Several different trips are available, each with a different theme and location. All tours provide a chance to see a diversity of native wildlife and offer a comfortable platform for photography. 239.530.594

TREASURE SEEKERS - Specializing in shelling tours for the serious shelling enthusiast and casual collector, Captains Tammy and Jeff Everts operate a brand new 2018, 24 ft SeaPro bayboat equipped with a freshwater shower and bathroom. Four hour, small group tours for up to six people, and custom full day tours for maximum privacy, are scheduled based on daily tides for optimal shelling. Each tour concludes with a visit to the famous dome home at Cape Romano. Leaving from Goodland Boating Park. 239.571.2331

Fun Boat Trips

BLACK PEARL PIRATE SHIP CRUISES -This popular boat, offers interactive kid's pirate-themed tours and 1½ hour sunset cruises with DJ, dancing on deck and a full bar. Also offering private charters. Leaving from Rose Marina, 951 Bald Eagle Dr. 239.404.5422.

CAPTAIN PARTY HARD - Boat like a Local, Party like a Rock Star! Adults Only, 21 years+. Departing Marco Island twice daily on board a beautiful 27 foot Hurricane deck boat for a 3.5 hour boat/beach party. Vessel includes a bathroom, beverages and snacks complimentary. Everything you need to have fun like you live here is provided - beach chairs, games, beverages and snacks; all you need is a towel and to be ready to have fun! 239.235.9414

MARCO PEDAL BOAT - The Marco Pedal Boat is a brand new 31-foot long catamaran, propelled through the water by a large rear paddle powered by the pedaling of passenger riders. The boat, which leaves from Caxambas Park three times a day, for a two hour tour with a master captain and first mate, can accommodate up to 16 guests. Pedaling passengers' seats are arranged around a central bar with built in LED cup holders. There's also additional seating at the front for those who don't want to pedal or want to take a break. Bring your own drinks and snacks so you can sip and cycle. 239.920.1230

THE SCREAM MACHINE - The thrill of a roller coaster, with the excitement of white water rafting! The Scream Machine – a one-hour jet boat thrill ride - arrived on Marco recently and departs daily from the Goodland Boat Park at 11.00 am, 1.00 pm, 3.00 pm and Sunset. She is a Smoky Mountain, New Zealand style jet boat, 30' long and weighing in at over five tons. Twin turbo-charged engines push her along at over 40 knots! Up to 23 guests will enjoy 360° full speed spins, power slides, hair-pin turns and nose dives. Children must be at least 38" tall to enjoy the ride. 317-709-2235

Sailboat Tours

COOL BEANS CRUISES Whatever your sailing or boating pleasure, Cool Beans Cruises go the extra mile to make it happen. Whether your interests are nature, relaxation, shelling or sightseeing, their goal is to bring your vision to life. Aboard one of their two beautiful catamarans, one accommodating up to six guests and the other up to 20 guests, they create the perfect sailing experience. Choose from their 3 hour day sails or a 2.5 hour champagne sunset cruise. The price is $65/person + tax (credit price) or $60/person (cash price). Departing daily from Isles of Capri Marina. Visit their site to learn more. 239-777-0020.

SWEET LIBERTY - Set sail from Naples City Dock on the area's largest sailing catamaran! Make a day of it and enjoy Naples' unique attractions. Bring your own cooler for your favorite beverage/picnic and enjoy island shelling, narrated nature cruises, beautiful sunsets and admire the spectacular homes of the Naples Bay area. USCG licensed for up to 44 passengers (it even has two bathrooms!). Please call to compare rates and times.   880 12th Avenue S, Naples. 239-793-3525

Waverunner Tours

AVI'S WATER SPORTS - Avi Langer, one of Marco Island's most experienced, enthusiastic and well loved waverunner tour guides, has recently set up his own water sports company and invites you to come and enjoy a safe, fun, family orientated tour of the 10,000 islands with him.   Avi, also known as the dolphin whisperer, knows the local dolphins and backwaters intimately and offers 2½ hour tours, with a maximum of three waverunners, accommodating up to two adults and one child per machine.   Avi, a keen photographer, will give you a CD of the photos he takes during your tour and can also provide additional professional photography on request. Two scheduled tours leave from Caxambas Boat Park daily and he also offers sunset and/or private tours on request. 239.777.9873

CAPT. RON'S AWESOME EVERGLADES ADVENTURES - 2½ hour guided waverunner excursions deep into the 10,000 islands with SW Florida's most experienced waverunner guide. Capt. Ron's is the only local tour company that deploys an underwater microphone when encountering a pod of vocal dolphins and this allows those on the tour to hear the dolphins communicating between themselves. Dry departures from Caxambas Park, hassle-free parking, deluxe machines, souvenir pictures and GPS tracking are just some of the other extra features of these trips. 239-777-9975

FLORIDA ADVENTURES AND RENTALS - Guided jet ski tours deep into the 10,000 islands, where no boat can venture. Guaranteed dolphin sightings or your money back! Cape Romano is one of the many stops along the 30 mile route. From the Gulf of Mexico and into the pristine estuaries of the 10,000 Islands, you will see an array of wildlife that will keep you captivated the entire time. Tours leave from Caxambas Marina on the south end of Marco Island. Jet skis hold up to 3 guests (450 lbs max). If you prefer to go it alone, they also offer jet ski rentals. 239.348.5551

MARCO ISLAND JET SKI TOURS & RENTALS - provide guided jet ski tours through the backwaters of the 10,000 islands to the dome home at Cape Romano and into the Gulf of Mexico, starting at $150. Also catering to groups and corporate events. Arrange free pick up at your hotel or Marco Island home. Tours leave daily from Caxambas Park. Fully insured, certificates available on request. 239.888.2488

MARCO ISLAND WATERSPORTS - Waverunner rentals and guided waverunner tours through the 10,000 Islands mangrove forest and the sparkling waters of the Gulf of Mexico. See dolphins, manatee and many wading birds at close quarters. Leaves from the beach in fine weather or from Calusa Marina in Goodland when the Gulf is rough but the backwaters are calm. Call 239.389.4FUN.

Other On the Water Options

Cruises

KEY WEST EXPRESS - Save hours of driving by taking this relaxing three hour cruise on a jet powered vessel to Key West, either for the day or stay over and return another day. www.keywestexpress.net. Departs from Rose Marina, 951 Bald Eagle Dr. Marco Island. Map 1 (3C)   888-579-7805

FOXC CRUISES the ultimate in luxury private charters! This beautiful 43' Tiara Sovran motor yacht has A/C, full galley, multiple flat screen tvs, full restrooms and all the comforts of home. Departs from Rose Marina, 951 Bald Eagle Dr., Marco Island 239.537.4440

MARCO ISLAND PRINCESS - 90ft luxury cruise vessel, the Marco Princess, offering narrated sightseeing, luncheon, sunset, dinner and party cruises.   Daily departures from Rose Marco River Marina. 642-5415

Parasailing

MARCO ISLAND WATERSPORTS - the ultimate eco thrill! enjoy a birds eye view of the sparkling waters of the Gulf of Mexico, possibly seeing dolphin, manatee, fish and birds from on high. Leaving from the beach at the Marco Island Marriott Resort or the Hilton Beach Resort. Call 239.389.4FUN.

Guided Tours Not On the Water

Experience a breathtaking aerial sightseeing tour of Marco's beautiful beach and surrounding area (they can even go down to the Everglades!) or take an Everglades safari where expert guides will show you to all the best places to see alligators, rare birds like bald eagles, white pelicans and Roseate spoonbills and take you on guided nature walks so you can see this unique environment up close and personal, they also include airboat tours.

On Foot
EVERGLADES AREA TOURS - Guided walking, birding and photography tours, through the cypress swamps, sloughs and marl prairies of the Everglades, in search

of orchids, bromeliads, herons, egrets, owls, hawks, alligators and other reptiles. 239.204-5344

On Four Wheels
BILLY 'OS VANTASTIC TOURS - Join Billy O's Vantastic Tours of Marco Island for a trip to the Everglades. Enjoy a thrilling ride through the sawgrass marshes on a small airboat, a nature walk, visit a wildlife refuge and spot wildlife and birds on a nature drive through the Big Cypress Swamp. Learn the eco system and history of early inhabitants and settlers of this mysterious land. 239-394-7699.

ROCK RENTALS - Now offering informational Marco Island tours in six seater, street legal golf carts. Rock Rentals will pick you up from your location, and take you on a tour of the island, stopping at various sights of interest. Or let them be your designated driver on a narrated tour of the island or a local pub crawl to the islands' best spots for nightly entertainment. For more information see their facebook page at 239.908.6878

On Two Wheels

NAPLES BICYCLE TOURS - will take you off the well beaten track to experience the wonder of the Everglades. Get away from it all in a quiet and peaceful setting, surrounded by nature. Or join them on a scenic guided bicycle tour of Marco Island or Old Naples. 239.825.6344

SCOOTERTOWN - Scenic guided bicycle tours of Marco Island, Naples and the natural environment of the Everglades. 239.394.8400

Golf

SW Florida is famous for its wonderful golf courses, which are open year round, and there are literally hundreds of great ones in our area. Our closest full course is right here on the island at the beautiful full service

ISLAND COUNTRY CLUB. Like most of the clubs in our area, the Island Country Club it is a private course - call 239-394-6611 for membership details. Island Country

Club is closed over the summer for course renovations and will open again in December.

Here are a few suggestions of golf courses in Naples which are open to the public:
JW MARRIOTT'S GOLF CLUB AT MARCO, 793-6060
www.marcoislandmarriott.com
LELY FLAMINGO ISLAND & MUSTANG GOLF
CLUBS,793-2223   www.lely-resort.net
FOREST GLEN 354-1898 www.forestglengcc.com
EAGLE LAKES GOLF CLUB, 732-0034

www.eaglelakesgolfclub.net

Local driving ranges include:
CORAL ISLE GOLF CENTER, 732-6900

Adventure Golf
CORAL CAY ADVENTURE GOLF - Two 18 hole courses, also offers inflatable rentals. Open 7 days 10am-11pm. www.coralcaygolf.com. 2205 E. Tamiami Trail, Naples - 30 minutes from Marco. 239.793.4999

MARCO GOLF AND GARDEN - 18 hole miniature course in a tropical garden setting. Fun for kids and challenging for adults. Open 7 days, 10am-10pm. www.marcogolfandgarden.com. 971 Winterberry Dr.

Map 1 (8C). 239.970.0561

www.marcogolfandgarden.com

Bicycle, Scooter & Street Legal Golf Cart Rentals
Marco Island is a wonderful place to cycle, with several of our main roads having designated bike paths alongside them and many miles of flat, uncrowded roads.

DOLPHIN COVE MARINA - Bicycle rentals. 1135 Bald Eagle Drive. Map1 (2C) www.dolphincovemarina.com. 239.289.8654

ROCK RENTALS - These six seater street legal golf carts are a fun way to get around the island. Daily, weekly and monthly rentals are available and delivery on Marco is free. Check out their page at www.Facebook.com/rockrentalsllc. 239.908.6878

SCOOTERTOWN - Scooters, bikes, in-line skates, beach stroller and wheelchair rentals by the hour, day or week. Kids' bikes, baby seats and 4 wheeled surreys complete the line-up. 1095 Bald Eagle Dr. Map1 (3C) 239.394.8400 www.islandbikeshops.com

Spas, Beauty, Hair & Fitness

THE SPA HILTON MARCO ISLAND - full service spa - the perfect place to pamper, nurture, energize and soothe yourself. The emphasis is on personal service and the luxurious facilities include sauna, steam room, Vichy shower, relaxation lounges and spa garden. Reservations can be made on line and several different packages are available. Their gift certificates make wonderful gifts for friends, family or even yourself! - 560 South Collier Blvd, 239.642.2144

MARCO ISLAND YOGA - A mindful hour of yoga on Marco's beautiful south beach just south of the Apollo and Sunset Grille (use South Beach access). Everyone is welcome from beginners to accomplished yogis and if you don't have a mat just bring a beach towel and plenty of water. This is a fantastic location to practice yoga, with a great beach view. Bring the kids and make it a family affair. $10 suggested donation. Weather permitting, classes are Monday to Wednesday 5.30 to 6.30 pm and Thursday to Sunday 8.30 to 9.30 am. Every Tuesday from 6.30 pm, join in a guided meditation for 20 minutes. Debby, Megan and Laurie take turns in leading the class. Map1 (8C) Follow them on Facebook or call for more information...201.214.1360 / 712.210.3853

SALON & SPA BOTANICA - Whether your needs are relaxation, beautification or therapeutic, the team at Salon and Spa Botanica is committed to giving you exceptional customer service and will strive to provide you with an unforgettable salon and day spa experience. Their services include hair, nails, massage therapy, skin rejuvenation, electrolysis and wedding services. Specializing in dimensional Aveda Hair Color, Make-Up, complete makeovers and so much more. They are proud to be using only the finest professional and organic products that will beautify and balance both the body and mind bringing forth your own personal beauty and style without harming the environment... Beauty in Harmony with Nature. Shops of Marco, 141 S Barfield Dr.

www.salonandspabotanica.com. 239.394.6633

SASCHA'S SALON - This full service ladies' and men's hair salon specializes in precision cuts, long hair, color/hilites and men's color. Now also offering Botox and facial fillers with Anne Branstrator ARNP. Ownership by master colorist/stylist Maria Elena. 907 N. Collier Blvd, 239.394.3550 www.saschassalon.com

Services, Clubs and Classes

Home Builders
FREY & SON HOMES - combining taste, value and fine craftmanship - that's the key to a great custom home and this family have been building exquisite custom homes in SW Florida since 1972. Visit their Barbados model home at 861 N Barfield Dr.

 www.freyandson.com. 239.394.1964

SEA GLASS ARCHITECTURE - Bob Diericks and his wife Kasia have recently established this full service licensed architectural practice. With 30 years of professional experience, Bob was educated under the modernist school of Mies van de Rohe. Bob and Kasia (also a degreed architect) can bring a wealth of experience working various styles to each and every local residential and commercial project.
www.SeaGlassArchitecture.com. 239.BOB.DRAW

Photography
MARCO ISLAND PHOTOGRAPHY - For a wonderful memento of your Marco Island vacation why not have master photographer Peter Berec take a sunset portrait of your family on the beach?
www.marcophotography.com/. 239.642.3500.

Shipping
KEEP IN TOUCH - packing, boxes, shipping supplies and fruit shipping are available at this store, as well as a US Postal Office contract postal unit.

www.keepintouchstore.com Shops of Marco. Map 1 (6F) 239.393.630

SUNSHINE BOOKSELLERS - UPS, FedEx Shipping and crating with free local pickup when shipping through their account. www.sunshinebooksellers.com. 1000, N Collier Blvd #14 Map1 (4C). 239.394.5343

THE UPS STORE - avoid airport hassles by getting your excess luggage packed and shipped home ahead of time by the UPS store. Marco Town Center Mall. Map1 (4C), 239.642.0011

Transportation
A-CLASS TRANSPORTATION at your service! Luxury, service and affordability in airport transportation.www.aclasstransportation.com. 239.389.0550

CANARY TRANSPORTATION - established in 2005, specialize in trips from Marco to all south Florida airports in clean, comfortable and reliable vehicles. From one to seven passengers, and more if necessary, courteous drivers are dependable and on time. Weddings, proms, business meetings and a night on the town in addition to their airport service. www.canarytransportation.com 239.325.7207

ROCK RENTALS - six and eight seater, street legal golf carts. Daily weekly and monthly rentals available. Free delivery to anywhere on the island. Now offering informational Marco Island tours - Rock Rentals will pick you up from your location, and take you on a tour of the island, stopping at various sights of interest. Or let them be your designated driver on a local pub crawl to the islands' best spots for nightly entertainment. For more information, see their facebook page at www.Facebook.com/rockrentalsllc/ 239.908.6878

 SALT LIFE TRANSPORTATION - provide fast, friendly, professional airport trips at a fair price. It also offers $7 rides anywhere on Marco from 5pm-1am Tuesday thru Thursday and from 5pm - 3am Friday & Saturday and a Stan's Sunday Funday shuttle service (see their ad on Page 73 for details). And, for a limited time it is offering complimentary shuttle service (tip only), to and between the Marco Island restaurants listed on the restaurant map on (excludes Goodland and Capri) during the hours given above. The ride home is just $7. www.saltlifetransportation.com 239.308.8686

Pool Service & Repair
GB POOLS - call Marco Islander George Baran for a free quote for reliable weekly swimming pool maintenance and expert pool equipment installation and repairs. Ask about his special offer for Marco Review readers!   www.GBPoolsMarcoIsland.com 239.249.1107

Local Airport
MARCO AIRPORT - The Marco Island Executive Airport is conveniently located to Marco Island, Naples, Goodland and Isles of Capri and provides "red carpet service" for tourists, clients and residents flying privately into and out of SW Florida. It provides affordable, convenient, safe hassle-free air travel. Airport staff provides professional, friendly, personal

service to all customers and arranges for ground transportation and local reservations upon request. A $9.4 million project is currently underway which includes a new aviation terminal expected to be in operation by the spring of 2019 after which demolition will begin on the existing facilities.

Clubs & Organizations
MARCO ISLAND RACQUET CLUB - The only publicly available tennis, pickleball and racquetball facility on Marco Island. Outdoor, lighted courts and air-conditioned, indoor racquetball courts available year-round. Members and non-members alike are welcomed. Racquets and paddles are available for loan at no cost with a court rental or guest fee. Daily, no-fee court time available weekly. Call for current court availability, reservations and scheduled activities. 1275 San Marco Rd., 239.394.5454

RESIDENTS' BEACH - open to Marco Islanders who own improved property or rent for a month or longer (30-59 day rentals from January 1 through April 30 qualify for walk-on Residents' Beach/park at Sarazen Park membership only). www.marcocivic.com. 1770 San Marco Road, Suite 204. 239.642.7778.

Classes
MARCO ISLAND CENTER FOR THE ARTS - Offering a whole range of classes for adults and children. www.marcoislandart.org 1010 Winterberry Drive. 239.394.4221

MALENDA TRICK - Art lessons by appointment. Shops of Olde Marco 258 Royal Palm Drive. 239.394.2787

MARCO ISLAND YOGA - daily yoga classes on south beach. Marco Map (8C). for more information, (201) 214.1360 / (712) 210.3853

Restaurants

Whether you are looking for the freshest local seafood, a view of the water from your table, live music to dance the night away or a once in a lifetime, special occasion celebration, there is a local restaurant that fits the bill. Here in our Restaurant Review we have broken down dining choices into four categories to make chosing your dining destination simple.

Island Chic

Fine dining at its best. The food and experience at these locally owned island favorites are worth leaving the beach for.

CAFE DE MARCO "Live to Savor!" Nestled in the charm of Olde Marco's Historic District, one of the island's finest seafood restaurants is celebrating 34 years of culinary excellence. The vast wine selection, award winning seafood and chef created specialities guided by the principles of sustainability) and the outstanding service will ensure a truly satisfying evening out. Voted best seafood on Marco since 1983 and awarded Certificate of Excellence from 2011-2017. Twilight specials at $14.95 (available 5-5:45pm), except on holidays. 244 Palm Street, Olde Marco. Restaurant Map (2) 239-394-62622 ww.cafedemarco.com. Don't Miss: Their signature broiled Jumbo Prawns - delicious!

RISTORANTE DA VINCI'S - Experience the charm of Italy without the jet lag! Sophisticated taste blends into a family atmosphere where each guest will feel at home while enjoying signature dishes and carefully selected wines. The marble interior is RISTORANTE DA VINCI'S (continued) complemented by mosaics, a mural of Leonardo Da Vinci's artwork and a full indoor/outdoor bar. Enjoy sushi prepared from the freshest ingredients before your eyes. Lunch and dinner are served daily and the bar, with its wood-burning pizza oven, stays open late. Don't miss DJ night, Friday and Saturday from 10pm, playing sounds from the 80s, 90s and modern day. New "Quiet Room", with conference facilities, available for private groups and parties. 599 S Collier Blvd, Marco Walk, across from the Hilton Hotel. Restaurant Map (7) 389-1888
www.ristorantedavinci.com   Known for: Authentic Italian Pasta and wood-burning pizza oven

THE DECK AT 560 BAR & RESTAURANT - located in Hilton Marco Island Beach Resort and Spa, features a stunning indoor and outdoor dining room that overlooks the Gulf of Mexico with its magnificent sunsets. Open for breakfast, lunch and dinner daily with a great happy hour. The menu focuses on seafood from local waters as well as meat and produce from their own beach-side garden and local farms. 560 S. Collier Blvd. Restaurant Map (8) 239-642-2181.

On The Water.

Known for: Craft cocktails with a magnificent sunset view

FIN BISTRO - Husband and wife team Brian and Kathy O'Brien opened this casual restaurant, which focuses on fresh and locally caught fish, in 2012 and it quickly became a firm favorite with islanders and visitors alike. Last summer they moved in with their sister restaurant Ohana and now offer a full bar in their new larger location and live music with Sky Jammer on Wednesday and Thursday evenings. Reservations recommended. Open for dinner from 5.30pm Tuesday-Saturday. Closed for vacation June 2nd-18th. 657 S.

Collier Blvd. www.finbistro.com. 317 N. Collier Blvd,. Restaurant Map (9)   239-970-6064. Known for: Local fresh seafood specials

LA TAVOLA - American Bistro. Come Gather at The Table! Farm to table concept restaurant using only the freshest ingredients. Serving fresh wild caught seafood, prime organic meats, organic greens, local farm produce and homemade desserts. Open for lunch and dinner seven days. Join them in the lounge bar for signature crafted cocktails and an extensive wine list with happy hour daily from 11am-6pm and happy hour food 3-6pm as well as live entertainment seven days from January. Full menu available in the bar. Reservations recommended, Outdoor Seating Available. Check their site or Facebook page for more information. www.latavolarestaurantandbar.com. 961 Winterberry Drive. Restaurant Map (10)   239-393-4960. Don't Miss: The happy hour and live entertainment in the lounge

MANGO'S DOCKSIDE BISTRO - tropical dining in a beautiful waterside setting at the Esplanade. The decor is colorful and fun with outside seating and an amazing view of Smokehouse Bay. Serving creative breakfasts, lunches and dinners with Sushi from 12 noon-9pm daily. Call for live entertainment schedule, don't miss their fabulous tropical cocktails and check out their new salt water fish tank! Happy hour 3-7pm daily, take-out and exceptional catering. Open Monday - Sunday 8am - 9pm. Please visit www.mangosdocksidebistro.com for full menus. The Esplanade, 760 N Collier Blvd. Restaurant Map (13) 239.393.2433. On The Water: Don't Miss: Sipping the Smokehouse Bay Martini overlooking Smokehouse Bay

MARCO PRIME - One of Marco's chicest new restaurants. Although the decor is upmarket, the ambiance is friendly and relaxed. The menu offers a combination of a-la-carte, with a choice of a dozen sides and sauces to accompany your meat or fish selections, and all-inclusive house specialties. The extensive wine list features over two dozen wines available by the glass. The popular outside bar, which extends out into the pretty, well-shaded courtyard, also serves the full menu. The Carvelli family (of Restaurante Da Vinci fame) has used their many years of experience to create a comtemporary steak and seafood house with all the warmth and attention to detail you have come to expect from them. Marco Walk Plaza 599 S. Collier Blvd #304 Restaurant Map (15) 239.389.2333 www.marcoprime.com Don't Miss: Happy Hour at the outdoor bar & patio

THE OYSTER SOCIETY - Bringing 1920s glamor and sophistocation to Marco in a casual and comfortable setting, combining a "Great Gatsby" theme with a nautical fusion. Offering a wide selection of fresh local seafood, shellfish and daily raw bar specials, and complemented by a first class wine list and hand-crafted cocktails, this restaurant is definitely here to stay. Located in Marco Walk near its sister restaurants Marco Prime and DaVinci, The Oyster Society is dedicated to giving each guest a memorable experience while celebrating innovative ways prepare the fresh ingredients. www.theoystersociety.com 599 S. Collier Blvd., Marco Walk. Restaurant Map (19) 239-394-33474 Don't Miss: Fresh seafood, great happy hour & live entertainment

SALE E PEPE - Enjoy breathtaking views of the Gulf of Mexico while dining on elegant Italian cuisine at the award-winning Sale e Pepe restaurant. A celebration of Italian cuisine, architecture and décor, Sale e Pepe features the culinary traditions of southern Italy updated and complemented by South Florida's fresh produce and seafood for a menu beyond compare. Sale e Pepe's intimate dining room features hand-painted frescos, intricate tile mosaics and Roman arches framing private dining nooks while the outdoor Terrace offers stunning views of the Gulf of Mexico and its famed sunsets. Plus, enjoy a selection from our 400 label wine list, consistently recognized by Wine Spectator magazine with its Best of Award of

Excellence. Daily Happy Hour 4:30-6pm. Open nightly for dinner. Reservations suggested. Located at Marco Beach Ocean Resort, 480 S. Collier Boulevard. Restaurant Map (21) 393-1600 www.sale-e-pepe.com. ON THE BEACH

Known For: Fine dining with a view of the beach

Laid Back

True Marco Island style. Laid back and comfortable. Enjoy any of these casual restaurants for their relaxed atmosphere and quality food and service.

CAPRI FISH HOUSE RESTAURANT Fresh Florida seafood is the specialty in this casual family owned and operated restaurant where every seat has an amazing sunset view. The waterside chickee bar looks out onto beautiful Johnson Bay and a small sandy beach. Live entertainment. Sunday "all-you-can-eat" buffets - breakfast buffet from 9-11am and lunch/dinner buffet from 11:30-4:00pm. Early bird specials from 4-5:45pm Daily. Happy hour 2:30-5:30pm daily. Come see their brand new inside/outside bar and now offering a full bar! Special occasions and large parties welcome, major credit cards accepted. www.caprifishhouse.com, 203 Capri Blvd., Isle of Capri. Restaurant Map (3) . 239-389-5555.

ON THE WATER:

Don't Miss: The Sunday Breakfast and Lunch Buffets

COCOMO'S - Casual dining at its best! Relax while your kids play in their game room. Come and get a taste of what the Island is talking about. Marco's finest menu with the best variety. Serving incredibly fresh fish including Grouper, Yellowtail, Mahi, Ahi Tuna, (Tuna Nachos are a local favorite), Steaks (including a 14oz bone-in ribeye) Salads, Chicken lettuce wraps, Falafal and Hummus, Marco's best Grouper sandwich and many other great items. Don't forget the Cocomo Bread. Happy hour 3-6 daily. $4.99 Margaritas and $2.99 16oz selected drafts all day everyday. Serving Lunch: Mon-Fri from 11:30-4:00 and Dinner: Mon-Fri 4:00-close, Sat-Sun 5:00-close. "U Hook it, We'll Cook it!" Ask about daily food specials and their whole tempura fried hogfish! 945 N. Collier Blvd (between McDonald's and Bald Eagle in Sunset Plaza) Restaurant Map (4)   394-3600 www.cocomosgrill.com. Known For: Whole tempura fried hogfish and consistent good quality

CRABBY LADY – This waterside restaurant was named after owner Captain Cameron's boat and used to be a bait store many years ago. Located directly on Marco River in Goodland,

the Crabby Lady combines one of the best views around with fresh local seafood. With blue crabs from their own boat and local seafood delivered daily, the menu is simple but delicious. Outside seating by the river or in the open porch adds to the relaxed Florida style atmosphere. Live music Thursday thru Sunday. Open Tuesday to Sunday from 8am for breakfast, with lunch starting at 11am. Now serving dinner Tuesday to Saturday til 9pm.   Happy hour from 3 to 7pm. www.crabbylady.com 123 Bayshore Way, Goodland.

Restaurant Map (5) 239. 500.CRAB.

Known for: Old Florida feel and fresh seafood

LITTLE BAR - Located right on the water in the quaint fishing village of Goodland, Little Bar, a local tradition for 39 years, continues to serve consistently good seafood and steaks in a relaxed and friendly atmosphere. Varied menu. Fresh Seafood including Grouper, Soft Shell Crab, Stone Crab Claws, Steaks and Prime Rib, luncheon and dinner specialties, as well as traditional waterfront fare. Open seven days at 11:30, dinner service begins at 5. Attitude Adjustment 3-6. Eat indoors, on the screened lanai or in the casual leafy surroundings of the waterside patios. The Best Live Entertainment in the intimate bar. Get there by bike, boat or Bugatti. www.LittleBarRestaurant.com.

Goodland. Restaurant Map (12) Friend them on Facebook 394-5663

ON THE WATER

Don't Miss: Papa Ray's chocolate peanut butter pie. Just trust us, it's good!

MARCO ISLAND PRINCESS - Marco's on the water lunch and dinner dining experience! Help yourself to a delightful lunch or dinner, while enjoying the sights of Marco by water or a spectacular Gulf sunset. The "Marco Island Princess" accommodates up to 149 passengers and offers two full service bars. Reservations Recommended. Cruises depart from Rose Marina. Restaurant Map (14)

www.themarcoprincess.com. 642-5415.

LITERALLY ON THE WATER!

Known For: Giving 'on the water' dining a whole new meaning!

MARGARITA'S Serving authentic Mexican cuisine for lunch, dinner, take-out and now delivery. Margarita's promise is to serve the best Mexican food you've ever tasted! Daily happy hour 3-6pm. Outside seating on the patio and inside seating in restaurant and Margarita bar. Follow them on Facebook and Twitter. Order take-out or delivery by phone or on-line. Marco Town Center Mall, 1069 N Collier Blvd. Restaurant Map (16)

For take-out or delivery call 394-6555.

www.margaritasontheisland.com

Known For: Authentic Mexican dishes, and their reliable delivery service and Cinco de Mayo party

NACHO MAMA'S - With indoor and shaded outdoor seating, this restaurant offers a wide menu of Tex-Mex and American dishes. Favorites include their tuna tower appetizer, shrimp, chicken and beef combo fajitas, and their fabulous grande nanchos, enough to feed the whole family! Open 11am-1am 7 days, (kitchen open 'til midnight). Two great happy hours daily 3pm & 10pm-close, except on nights with entertainment. Don't miss their St Patrick's Day party on March 17th and Cino de Mayo on May 5th with live bands in the plaza 3-10pm and DJ inside from 10pm-1am. Live entertainment with the Elliot West Band Saturday nights and Mark Thompson Sunday 6-9pm. 599 South Collier Blvd. Marco Walk, across from the Hilton. Restaurant Map (18).

www.thenachomamas.com. 389-2222.

Don't Miss: Nacho Mama's World Famous Margaritas & St Patrick's Day and Cinco de Mayo parties

PARADISE FOUND RESTAURANT & BAR - One of the areas's most picturesque waterfront restaurants, offering panoramic views of the Marco River and Goodland Bay from its newly enlarged outside deck and inside restaurant and lounge. Built in 1869 by W D Collier as his family home on Marco, it was moved to its present location in 1965. The menu offers a wide variety of shellfish and seafood with a popular salad bar. Come by boat or car, see the mermaids at the weekend, and enjoy the regular live entertainment (see The Marco Review App for details). Free parking lot shuttle. Open 7 days, 11:30 to close. 401 Papaya St, Goodland. Restaurant Map (20) 239-330-7773

ON THE WATER

Don't Miss: Their live entertainment with great water views

SAMI'S PIZZA | PASTA | GRILL - Sami's has undergone a huge transformation over the last year and is now a fully fledged great value family restaurant with an inside/outside bar. As well as the delicious thin crust pizza, by the slice and by the pie, they are famous for, they now serve a full menu of dishes from around the world, including a delicious lunch time Mexican build your own taco bar. Live entertainment seven nights in season. Delivery is free to your home, hotel or condo on Marco (minimum order required). On Goodland and Isles of Capri a delivery fee and minimum order will apply, please call for more info..Full menu available at www.samispizza.com. 227 N Collier Blvd. Restaurant Map (23) 239.389.7499.

Known For: The largest pizza on Marco Island and their fast delivery

SAND BAR - For over 30 years, Marco's family friendly sports bar has been"Where the locals go for consistently good food at reasonable prices". All the best sports packages, so catch your favorite team on one of over 40 TVs with new portable table speakers! Two pool tables, arcade games, kid's menu as well as free Wifi. Open every day with a full service bar and restaurant from 7am-2am, serving breakfast, lunch, dinner and late night. Three great happy hours. Live entertainment, Texas Hold'em on Mondays and free DJ Trivia on Wednesdays. No reservations needed. ATM on site. All major credit cards accepted. Take out available. www.sandbarmarco.com. 826 E Elkcam Circle, located behind Walker's Marine. Restaurant Map (24) 239-642-3625

Don't Miss: Their great new menu items like lobster and lamb chops

SNOOK INN - This iconic waterside Marco Island restaurant offers outdoor and indoor casual dining overlooking the beautiful Marco River. After 32 years under the same ownership, the restaurant sold in late 2017 and is now part of the Carvelli Restaurant Group, who also own island favorites Da Vinci's, Marco Prime and the Oyster Society. Enjoy their newly extended outside chickee bar, their newly refurbished inside restaurant with its famous salad bar and a wide variety of seafood, steaks, sandwiches and continental specialties as you watch dolphin, manatee and the boating activities. Come by car or boat, docks available. Live entertainment daily at the chickee bar. Happy Hour 4-6pm Mon-Fri and 10pm-close 7 days. Open 7 days 11am-10pm. 1215 Bald Eagle Drive. Restaurant Map (25) 394-3313 www.snookinn.com

ON THE WATER

Don't Miss: Daily entertainment outside by the chickee bar

STILTS As its name suggests, Stilts sits high above the sea grapes with a commanding view of the beach and Gulf of Mexico. Open for lunch and dinner, featuring their new locally inspired menu. Enjoy daily happy hour specials such as shrimp ceviche, crab nachos and watermelon and feta salad from 5.00 to 7.00 pm. You won't want to miss their breathtaking sunset view. Situated overlooking the beach at Marriott's Crystal Shores, 600 S Collier Blvd. 239.393.6800.

Don't miss: Happy Hour special appetizers and cocktails overlooking the beach

SUNSET GRILLE - Marco's only sports beach bar is celebrating its 11th anniversary. Enjoy a fabulous view of the beach while sipping a cocktail or sampling the wide ranging menu, which includes burgers, wings, steaks, seafood and pasta and a whole lot more. Locals and visitors gather for the daily happy hour at the tropical tiki bar while the sun sinks into the Gulf. If you prefer to dine in air-conditioned comfort there's a large indoor dining room with a spectacular gulf sunset view from any seat. Play shuffleboard or watch the many TVs for live sport. 900 South Collier Blvd., in the Apollo condominiums - ½ mile south of the Hilton. Also accessible from the beach. Restaurant Map (26) 389-0509 www.sunsetgrilleonmarcoisland.com

ON THE BEACH

Known For: Cocktails at sunset and great beach view

THE SPEAK EASY OF MARCO ISLAND - If you're looking for a friendly and fun place to relax, have a cocktail and enjoy some fresh, well prepared food, this restaurant with its brick, granite and neon rich interior and pretty waterside patio is a great place to start. Open from 11am for lunch and dinner 7 days. Call your order in for pickup or bring in your fresh catch for them to prepare for you. There's a full bar, Sport Packages - come watch your favorite teams - and don't miss their daily happy hour from 2-6pm. Johnny Fusco appears live every Saturday from 5-8pm and on Thursday there's karaoke from 6-9pm.Check site for details of specials. On and off premises catering available. Call Cindy to plan your next event. Come and visit their new retail store and take out area.

www.speakeasymarco.com.   1106½ N Collier Blvd., Restaurant Map (28)   239.970.2929.

ON THE WATER

Known For: Friendly neighborhood bar atmosphere

TOKYO INN - Your favorite Japanese Steak House and Sushi Bar. Tempura, seafood, traditional Japanese cuisine prepared before your eyes. Japanese hot and cold Sake and beer. Takeout can be ordered by fax, 642-1897.   1825 San Marco Road, Shops of Marco. Restaurant Map (30)   642-3999

Known For: Hibachi cooking at your table - a delight for young and old

TRIAD SEAFOOD CAFE & MARKET - This rustic family owned and operated restaurant in the heart of Everglades City serves the freshest of seafood on a deck over the beautiful Barron River. The view is spectacular and there is full table service. They also serve beer and wine and their key lime pies and sauces are homemade. "All-u-can eat" stone crab claws fresh from local boats are cooked on the premises when they're available. They are closed for a lot of the summer so please call first. Located in Everglades City behind the school on the Barron River. www.triadseafoodmarketcafe.com. 239-695-2662

ON THE WATER

Known For: Friendly laidback atmosphere and all you can eat stone crab claws

ZAZA - Recently opened intimate traditional Mexican taqueria, crafting authentic tacos and Latin Fusion street fare using high quality fresh ingredients. Taqueria-style tacos, fajitas and burritos with meat slowly cooked in their own smoker for 12 hours - even the vegetables for the homemade salsa are smoked. Serving Mexican beers, Sangria and ZaZaritas, ZaZa's own take on a margarita, complete with dry ice for a unique presentation. Happy hour every day from 3-5:30pm. Serving breakfast, lunch and dinner seven days. www.eatatzaza.com 1095 Bald Eagle Drive. Restaurant Map (32) 239-970-5205

Known for: great homemade guacamole and chips

T-Shirts & Flip Flops

For those days when all your extra minutes are spent on the beach or by the pool, these great restaurants don't mind your flip flops and t-shirts.

CRAZY FLAMINGO. Located at the Marco Town Center Mall, in the heart of Marco Island, the famed, Crazy Flamingo is a local favorite for casual fare including seafood, wings, burgers and more. Come as you are to Marco's only raw bar and sample fresh oysters and clams on the half shell shucked to order, succulent stone crabs (when in season) and their famous steam pot, chock-full of clams, mussels and oysters steamed in their own juices with secret spices, celery and onion. Enjoy live entertainment on weekends, billiards and the happiest happy hour twice a day every day from 3-5pm and again from 10pm-close. Great day at sea? Awesome! Bring in your fresh, filleted catch and they'll cook it up for you family style with Caesar salad and french fries. Serving Marco Island since 1989 and affectionately known to the locals as "The Bird Bar", The Crazy Flamingo, serving beer and wine inside and out is open daily from 11am-2am. Call ahead to order pick-up.. www.thecrazyflamingo.com. Marco Town Center Mall, 1035 N Collier Blvd.,

Restaurant Map (6) 239.642.9600

Don't Miss: The fresh shellfish steampot!

RED ROOSTER - One of Marco's most popular breakfast/lunch spots, with locals and residents alike. The light and airy restaurant is famous for its friendly atmosphere and perfectly cooked, freshly prepared housemade comfort food. Lunch treats include a selection of homemade quiches and tasty salads. www.redroostermarco.com. Like them at Facebook.com/redroostermarcoisland to see daily specials and more. Shops of Marco, 1821 San Marco Road. Restaurant Map (21) 239-394-3100.

Don't Miss: The assortment of daily quiche specials (especially the lobster!)

TAKE-OUT

Many Marco restaurants allow their full menu to be ordered as take-out, but Michelbob's Championship Ribs is purely a call-ahead and pick-up location

MICHELBOB'S ON MARCO - Winner of "Best Ribs in America" and numerous national and international "Best" Awards. This is the take-out version of the world famous restaurant in Naples. Featuring imported baby back ribs from Denmark and BBQ chicken, pulled pork, smoked sausage and a delicious selection of sides. Try their NEW short and meaty St. Louis Ribs and authentic Cuban Sandwiches. Open 7 days a week - all year long. Check site www.michelbobs.com for current hours. 915 North Collier Blvd.

Restaurant Map (17) 394-0302 www.michelbobs.com Known For: Reliable, call ahead delicious take-out dinners.

Sweet Treats & Coffee

Whether you are just starting your day, needing an afternoon pick-me-up, or an after dinner sweet treat, these locally owned Marco staples are the perfect destination to satisfy everyone in your group.

BEEBE'S ICE CREAM - - Located in Marco Walk close to the Movie Theater, this popular store offers 44 flavors of homemade ice cream and is the only ice cream store on Marco serving soft serve. Open Sunday-Thursday 1-11pm, Friday & Saturday 1-12pm. 599 S Collier Blvd. Restaurant Map (1) www.beebesicecream.com 239-

642-9800

Known For: A great spot to stop after Marco Movies

SWEET ANNIE'S -Serving ice cream the "old fashioned" way, at a sit down soda fountain, since 1986. Come indulge in their 47 flavors of ice cream, sorbet, frozen yogurt, and play a few games in the game room. Don't forget to check out their great selection of nostalgic candies, Marco Island and Florida souvenirs. Pint and quart pre-packed ice cream and ice cream pies are now also available to take home. Marco Islands #1 rated Ice Cream Shop. 692 Bald Eagle Dr. Restaurant Map (27) 642-7180.

Known For: The AMAZING traditional banana splits

WAKE UP MARCO - a friendly neighborhood coffee shop serving THE most delicious organic handcrafted coffees, as well as a great selection of teas. Bakery items such as muffins, bagels, croissants and pastries, are locally sourced, non gmo, organic and low in sugar, although they're so good you'd never guess it from their taste. It's the kind of place where, if you go in more than a couple of times, owner/barrista Oscar Galvez will spot you in the parking lot and have your favorite coffee brewing before you even open the door! www.WakeUpMarcoIsland.com 912 N Collier Blvd., Restaurant Map (31) 239-248-9398.

Don't Miss: The organic handcrafted cappuccinos and fresh muffins

For The Night Owls

Although locals affectionately refer to 9pm as "Marco Midnight" when everyone is tucked up in bed, there are some residents and many visitors who like to live it up! So, there are a few restaurants and bars that cater to these late night owls.

NACHO MAMA'S in Marco Walk have live entertainment late on Saturdays and their kitchen stays open every night until midnight.

Also in Marco Walk, DA VINCI'S has a DJ late Friday and Saturday nights.

Just across Winterberry Drive at LA TAVOLA, there's often late night entertainment in the lounge and bar as well as a lite bar menu.

In Marco Town Center Mall, CRAZY FLAMINGO, is open until 2am with food available until 1.30am and THE SNOOK INN has a late night happy hour from 10pm until close. And finally, the SAND BAR is open until 2am with full menu available until midnight.

Accommodation

Hotels
The Boat House
A family owned and operated motel tucked away in Olde Marco. They have boat slips, a fishing pier and you can watch dolphins, manatee and fish on the Marco river. Minutes from the Gulf of Mexico. 20 rooms. 23-642-2400

Hilton Marco Island Beach Resort
AAA Diamond Resort with 310 sophisticated and spacious guest rooms and suites, luxury spa and beach

view dining. This hotel will be fully open by the end of March 2019 after a complete remodel of rooms, concierge, lobby and restaurants-239-394-5000 hiltonmarcoisland.com

Lakeside Inn
A cozy island getaway nestled between palm trees and a fresh water lake with a sparkling heated pool and affordable rates year found. Apporximately 1½ miles from the beach and within easy reach of many of the island's restaurants and shopping centers. 20 rooms. 239-394-1161 marcoislandlakeside.com

Marco Beach Ocean Resort
This AAA five diamond resort features casual and fine dining, a spa and fitness center, pool and hot tub, roof gradens and is directly on Marco's beautiful five mile white sand beach. 98 rooms. 239-393-1400
 marcoresort.com

Jw Marriott Marco Island
Marco's largest world class resort is nestled on beautiful Marco beach and offers several restaurants,

championship golf, a full service spa and a wide range of activities and amenities including upscale shops for men and women and a free-form fantasy pool with views of the Gulf. This hotel was relaunched in January 2017 as a JW Marriott. The new adult-only, 93 room Lanai Tower is now open. 239-394-2511

www.jwmarco.com

Olde Marco Island Inn & Suites
51 two-bedroom suites. Built in 1883, this historic Victorian-style Inn with pool and hot tub, combines old world charm with modern accommodations. Approximately 3 miles from the beach, adjacent to The Collection at Olde Marco. Two blocks from The Snook Inn. 239-394-3131 oldemarcoinn.com

Port of The Islands Resort & Marina
Just 20 minutes drive from Marco Island, Port of the Islands Resort is located in the heart of the Everglades. The resort has an oversized outdoor heated pool, full service marina and boat ramp and is within walking distance of kayaking, eco tours, boat rentals, charter

fishing and nature tours. 32 rooms. 239-394-3101 poiresort.com

Rental Homes/Condos

MARCO ESCAPES - finer Marco Island and Naples area vacation rentals.   Marco Walk, 599 S Collier Blvd., Suite 115. Map1(8C). 239-217-6300 www.marcoescapes.com

MARCO ISLAND VACATION PROPERTIES®   - providing seasonal rental services, for guests seeking to discover and rediscover Marco Island, since 1989. 239.393.2121 / 800.462.7264. www.MarcoVacation.com

Harborview. 239-642-9200 harborview.rentals.com

Island Escapes 239.642.0000 / 800.762.3222 www.iEscapeAway.com

Prudential 239-642-5400

A Note about Renting a Property on Marco Island...
There are a lot of things to consider when renting a property on Marco... is it close to the beach access?

can I walk to restaurants? does the deck get sun all day long? ...to name but a few!

Most Marco Island Rental homes have screen lanai areas to the rear of the property. These protect occupants from bugs and, in many cases enclose private heated pools, and/or hot tubs. Some homes are landlocked but many are situated on Marco's 90 miles of inland canals. Many have private docks where you can moor rental boats/waverunners. If a house is said to be "indirect access" it means that there are bridges between it and the Gulf of Mexico. "Direct access" it means the canal has no bridges between it and the Gulf so it is suitable for large boats and sailboats. Houses whose rear lanai areas face south or west are the most desirable for sunset views and maximum sun, especially in winter when cooler winds tend to come from the north.

So, although Marco is relatively small, it is still advisable to use the services of a rental agent with local knowledge to help you find the property that suits your needs. Also, if you use a local agent, they will have someone available to resolve any issues that may arise during your stay.

And, one final piece of advice... be aware that Marco has been discovered and the good rental properties get snapped up quickly - so make your booking as early as you can!

Recommended Real Estate Agents

We understand that there are over 600 realtors on Marco Island - close to one for every 30 residents! We're pleased to say that we haven't met them all, but we have met all of our recommended realtors and know that they provide good service and have a wide knowledge of Marco. If you're thinking of buying or selling property on the island you certainly don't need to search through all 600 realtors, as you're sure to find one to suit you from the list below...

PREMIER SOTHEBY'S INTERNATIONAL REALTY, Brock and Julie Wilson Presenting Marco's finest properties.

Mention The Marco Review for a free realty consultation.

www.brockwilson.premiersothebysrealty.com.

239.595.5983

PREMIER SOTHEBY'S INTERNATIONAL REALTY, Cathy Rogers Presenting extraordinary properties to discriminating buyers. Read her Realty Review below for Cathy's insights into Marco's complicated Real Estate marker. www.marcoareaexpert.com.

239.821.7926

REMAX AFFINITY PLUS, Joe Contarino 35 years of experience. www.marcobeachfront.com. 239.970.2477

RESULTS REALTY OF SOUTHWEST FLORIDA, INC., Michael J Vale, For all of your real estate needs. www.resultsrealtyswfl.com. 239.389.9300.

REMAX AFFINITY PLUS, Chris Sullivan A leader in the luxury real estate. market. Selling Maro's finest properties while always keeping her clients' best inerest in mind. www.marcoluxuryhomes.com. 239.393.2222

ANCHOR REAL ESTATE, Shari Fairchild, Long term Marco resident and active realtor since 2004 with over $29 million in sales. Helping you make your move to paradise. 239.289.1772

PREMIERE PLUS REALTY, Yasmin and Mike Castellano strive to exceed the expectations of their buyers and sellers and they are committed to finding the perfect dream home for each individual. 978.423.1621 | 239.784.1611

eXP REALTY LLC, Jason Peach and Tanya La Butte, the LP Group. Marco Island specialists serving the Marco Island and Naples area. 239.908.6878

Real Estate Review

Are you Ready to Call Marco Island Home?

After rebounding from a major hurricane our 2018 sales were not our normal cyclical sales patterns of the past. Our best quarter was our third quarter (summer time) which is normally our slow quarter. In the first quarter of 2018 the average sales price was DOWN only 2.79% and median sales price was DOWN only 2.36%, still not bad after a major hurricane. In our second quarter our average sales price was UP 7.24%, median sales price was UP .073%. The third quarter average sales price was UP 19.36%, median sales price was UP 12.63%, and finally our fourth quarter average sales price was UP 1.10%, median sales price was UP 17.42%! Only one thing to say and that is "Marco Strong"! I think we have rebounded quite well!

Whether you are buying or selling, now is a good time to do either on this beautiful island! If you're like most people who visit, you'll start dreaming of becoming a resident of this idyllic island. Wherever you choose to live on this beautiful paradise, you will be pleased to know that you are never far away from shopping, dining, beaches and entertainment!

Marco Island is the largest and only developed island in Florida's Ten Thousand Islands, and its pristine waters, beautiful coastlines and spectacular community feel attracts people from all over the world! Packed with great amenities and things to do, this 4 mile by 6 mile Island, developed in the 1960s, has something for everyone. The beautiful white sand beaches, great water sports, and over 90 restaurants and bars was rated the #1 Island in the United States by Trip Advisor and #4 in the world in 2014! Our resort island has definitely been "discovered" as the JW Marriott has completed its renovation, becoming one of the best 5 star hotels in the world! People come from all over to enjoy our fishing in the Ten Thousand Islands. If you have never taken an eco boat or kayak tour of the Ten Thousand Islands, you really need to. It is beautiful, educational and you can see dolphins, maybe some manatees and all types of wildlife!

Off season, our island has around 17,000 full time residents; in season it swells to around 40,000+. Season is always packed full of fun events if you could tear yourself away from the beach for long enough!

From the Seafood Festival to outdoor art shows, movies in the park, our popular farmers' market, and Mutts and Martinis at CJ's. Although our summer is undoubtedly quieter, there is still plenty to do. Many great exhibits at the Center for the Arts, daily yoga at south beach, our world class Historical Museum, fabulous July 4th beach party, monthly beach clean-ups and of course the ever popular outdoor music at the Esplanade every Thursday. The Marco Review app has all of the dates and times as well as a list in the print magazine!

Shopping abounds on Marco with mostly quaint mom and pop stores with plenty of retail options! Marco Island is a very safe and community oriented island. We have our own Police Department and Sheriff's Department with our crime rate virtually zero. Our schools are all "A" rated with lots of parent participation.

If you are like most people who have visited Marco Island, you never want to leave, and the good news is that you don't have to! There are many different types of properties for sale, and it's just a matter of finding the one that matches your style, personality, and budget. To find that property, you must get a little more specific in your lifestyle and your wants and needs. "How many square feet do I want?" "What are my 'must haves?'" "Do I want a home or condo?" "Do I want a water direct (no bridges) home or condo, so I can have a large vessel or sailboat?" What's your Style? Contemporary or traditional? Prefer to live on a golf course or beach? As long as you know what you want, we can zero in on it.

Let's take a look at the different areas...

Marco Island is split up into many different areas with a variety of spectacular homes. From cozy condos with unbelievable views of the Gulf of Mexico, Ten Thousand Islands and more, to sprawling estate homes that you have to see to believe. Luxury waterfront homes and luxury waterfront condos are all around; more than 80 percent of the island is actually on water.

Hideaway Beach - is a gated community located on the northern most tip of the island. This is a private community and the only place where you can have a house right on the beach. They have condos on the golf course, condos on the water, homes on the beach, homes on the golf course and inland homes. There is currently one home on the beach for sale, listed at $7.5M, and one beachfront lot for $4.5M. There are inland homes ranging from $710K to $3.75M depending on the location, and inland lots ranging from $115K to $750K. Condos on the beach are between $759K to $1.545M and inland condos range from $879K to $959K.

Cape Marco - is located in the southwestern tip of Marco Island, and has six separate high-rise towers featuring gorgeous, well-appointed condos ranging in size from 1,300 SF to penthouses that measure over 13,000 SF. Cape Marco is comprised of The Merida, Tampico, Monterrey, Cozumel, Belize and Vera Cruz. Each building has its own amenities. Most have their own fitness rooms, theaters, and gathering rooms and some also have boardrooms and guest suites available. Prices range, depending on view and size, from $769K – $3.497M.

The Estates Area - is located in the south end of the island, comprising of very large "estate homes", with large oversized lots, on water direct and close to the Ten Thousand Islands. Some inland homes as well. A lot of "Mega Homes" are located here, due to the size of the lots and beautiful views. Very private and peaceful area. Inland homes range from $579K - $1.8M. Water direct homes range from $1.299M - $7.2M, and water direct lots range from $750K - $4.995M, with water indirect lots ranging from $240K - $725K.

Old Marco - is at the northeast corner of the Island and was one of the first developed areas on Marco, as a quaint old fishing village. It now features spectacular condominium complexes and water direct homes. These homes and condos vary in prices depending upon location and size. There are some inland homes and condos as well as water direct homes and condos. Water direct condos range from $199K - $439K, and water direct homes from $975K - $4.75M. Inland condos start around $174K up to $330K. There are no inland homes currently for sale.

The River Area - is located in the northeast and this beautiful area is generally serene and peaceful. Because it is just a short distance to Naples by boat, it's the perfect place to be if you are ready to set sail! Water direct homes in the area start from $549K to $3.999M.

The South End - is one of the most desirable spots as it is within walking distance to shops and restaurants. Condos and homes are either inland or water direct. Inland condos start at $299K - $695K, water direct condos (most with boat slips) start at $319.9K - $625K. Water direct homes start at $875K - $4.995M and inland homes range between $485K to $625K.

The Tigertail Area - near the northern end of Marco Island, Tigertail Beach is a 31-acre stretch of land so people love to live close by. The beach offers water sports and has a lot of natural resources. The homes in this area are within walking/biking distance to the beach. It is comprised of water direct homes (no bridges) starting at $805K - $3.15M and inland homes range from $479K - $785K.

Condos - Beachfront condos with 1 to 4 bedrooms range in price from $255K - $9.9M, and Gulf front condos with 2 to 4 bedrooms range from $549K - $1.399M, and inland condos ranging from $112K - $695K.

As you can see, there are many different condos and homes to choose from on Marco, and I hope this helps clarify some of the area/types of condos and homes available on our beautiful island. As always, you can contact me or one of my colleagues to help with your search! - Written on 1/14/19

The End

CPSIA information can be obtained
at www.ICGtesting.com
Printed in the USA
LVHW091526151221
706277LV00004B/115

9 781673 919929